Each Branch, Each Needle

An Anecdotal Memoir

The Final Stories

H. A. Dorfman

Hamilton Books
A member of
The Rowman & Littlefield Publishing Group
Lanham • Boulder • New York • Toronto • Plymouth, UK

Copyright © 2010 by
Hamilton Books
4501 Forbes Boulevard
Suite 200
Lanham, Maryland 20706
Hamilton Books Acquisitions Department (301) 459-3366

Estover Road
Plymouth PL6 7PY
United Kingdom

Library of Congress Control Number: 2010920221
ISBN: 978-0-7618-5074-8 (paperback : alk. paper)
eISBN: 978-0-7618-5075-5

For Ethan, Owen & Riley,

Still & Yet Again

And — For Anita, for 50 Years of

Love, Loyalty, Understanding & Tolerance

And — for Melissa and Dan,

All of Whom Have Given Meaning To My Life

Beyond My Ability To Properly Express It

"What if the world is filled with stories? ---
we hear only a few, live fewer,
and most that we live or hear
solve nothing, lead nowhere; but the spruce

appears again, rooted in dreamed tears,
yes, each branch, each needle
its own true story, yours,
mine, ours to tell."

"Stories III"
William Heyen

Contents

Introduction

I am seventy-five years old now. There is much to be said about being this age, some good, some bad. Health is the key, I think. Physical and mental. My body has never been an asset to me; my mind, such as it is, still offers me an acceptable level of service.

I do not, as many people my age do, digest the newspaper's obituary page with my morning coffee. But I am well aware that contemporaries die every day, those who pass on because of age and related ailments. Those who have had more dramatic or tragic endings are part of the world's sad history, dying because of some terrible deprivation or warring that man has not yet figured out how to stop. Not before my appearance on this planet, not since.

But it is the death of a family member, an old friend, a former teammate or teaching colleague—or a contemporary who, as an entertainer or sports figure or politician held a place in my own personal history that elicits a distinctive response. These deaths have made me more aware of my own mortality.

I assure caring people who call and check in on me that my streak goes on. When they ask first heard that response, they were not sure what I was talking about. "Consecutive days alive," I explained.

The doctors who forecast to my parents that I might not make it to ten years of age, then twenty, then forty are all dead now. I do not celebrate the death of those men; I celebrate their lack of accuracy. And I celebrate the present, reminded by Kierkegaard, that when one fights the future, he has "a dangerous enemy."

But I also, in my own way, celebrate my past. So here I am—still—presently telling stories about that past, instead of spending my time trying to figure out the universe.

I still work with professional athletes, having made a vow—"an appointment with myself"—to continue my work as long as I am able to make sense to myself and my clients. My counsel is offered almost exclusively on the telephone and via e-mail, with a few visits to my home each year by the particularly needy.

As for my relationship with the world these days—beyond my family, few friends and clients—I seek to be "free of mobs and movements, free as only very wild things are both solitary and free." Loren Eiseley wrote that. So I am my own version of a wild thing.

Many memories also have freed themselves. Memories that had been hiding below the surface of my awareness, while I was writing the two previous volumes of this trilogy. They have now risen, for reasons of their own. I could not have rooted them out. Their stories are presented within the covers of this book, accompanied by other matters that also bubbled up to the surface of my consciousness—and convinced me of their relevance in my life. Stuff my family wants my grandsons to know.

No individual's collection of stories can be all-inclusive, course. Nor should they be. But in this book, along with the previous two, enough of them have been presented to suggest what has directed me to be whatever I was meant to be.

I hope they inform those wonderful boys and, perhaps, interest other readers.

1

He Used to Be a Monk

After fourteen years working for baseball teams—with the daily regimen of games, meetings and accompanying travails, the travel on planes, the nights in the dugouts and hotel rooms—my professional life changed rather significantly. I would still be working with baseball players, primarily with those who were clients of the pre-eminent representative—'agent' is the less lofty term—Scott Boras. Anita had made a complete recovery from the surgery necessitated by breast cancer. And I had recovered from my year with the Tampa Bay Devil Rays.

The change suited and satisfied me. Rather than being involved in the everyday dynamic and the group-think that created tensions, frustrations and much wasted energy, I could again be a 'lone wolf.' Anita had long before offered her view that I could "be happy living in a cave." She was somewhat perplexed during the early years of our marriage, living with someone who could be outgoing and animated, but who preferred a reclusive life. I had to tell her repeatedly that her perspective of me at the front of a classroom or on a field as a competitor or coach, or in a gathering that required outspoken opinions, was the prepotency of understanding over predisposition. The pussy cat acting like a lion. Was I soft and cuddly and purring? Not that kind of cat, perhaps. But independent and territorial: Leave me alone.

Every effective teacher has to be an actor. And I was just that, I told her: an actor. As I had told Jim Coburn on the phone years before, when he wanted to know, "Who are you, Harvey Dorfman?"—I am whoever is required at the particular moment. Now, if he had asked, "Who do you most want to be?" I might have answered, "A monk." This is not frivolous fancy. Even a real monk saw my monkish potential. Naturally, an explanation must be given.

While teaching Advanced Placement English at Burr & Burton Seminary in Manchester, Vermont—no longer an actual seminary at that point—the school's Headmaster came to my classroom and asked me to drop into his office. "Nothing urgent," he said. "But maybe something interesting."

As I sat before him, he told me of a call he had received from the Father Prior at the monastery not far from our school. The Carthusian Monastery at the top of Mt. Equinox in Manchester had been built in the late 1960's. The Carthusians are a cloistered, silent order. The call was not made to recruit me as a monk, much the shame.

Houghton Pearl, the school's Headmaster, wore a cushion-faced expression of amusement as he sat silently, digging in his ear with the end of an engraved, wooden letter opener. "Are you going to share something with me?" I asked impatiently. Visits to his office were always twice as long as necessity would require.

"Well," he stated, "Father Diamond from the monastery called with a request. He told me he needs a tutor: someone who has a strong background in literature." Here he paused for effect. "And who was worldly." This spoken with a fat grin. "I told him I had just the guy for him." He waited, hoping I would ask who the guy was. I did not.

"Are you interested?" he eventually asked. I told him I'd think about it. He said, "That would be rich: *you* tutoring a monk." An affable but presumptuous man, he presumed to know me well.

Three days later I sat in front of Father Diamond. The entrance to the road up the mountain was a couple of miles south of the school on Route 7. Getting to the entrance of the monastery required a seemingly interminable drive (it might be four miles) up a narrow, winding road to the top of the mountain. An amazing sight and an even more amazing site, this place. Nearer their God to be.

The Father was a small man, in his fifties, I estimated. Before the interview I was to have, he told me a bit about himself, to establish some informality. I was perfectly at ease, ready to enjoy this unique experience. Father Diamond told me he had served in the U.S. Navy and was a converted Jew. He offered me a few glimpses of his early years, then asked me to do the same for him. After those preliminaries were taken care of, he questioned me in a manner that might have been similar to that of a member of an examination board. I was perfectly honest, telling him of my non-affiliation with any religious order, my reluctance to accept the dogma they provided, my unsuccessful search for something that might have satisfied whatever spiritual yearning I had during my college years. I concluded this subject by expressing my disappointment and my evolving 'development' as a very skeptical agnostic.

After listening patiently and with apparent interest, he said. "I would like you to help me if you are willing to do so. First, I will tell you what I believe you must to know about my need. *Our* need—meaning Father Don Benedict's and mine." No compensation was mentioned, by either party. This was a *pro bono* deal with a loftier payoff, I decided.

The specific need to be addressed was Father Benedict's "lack of worldliness," as defined by the Father Prior. Don Benedict was the candidate of choice to become a Father Prior in the foreseeable future. A new monastery was being built in California and should Father Diamond preside there, Father Benedict would take his place on the summit of Mt. Equinox. The alternate possibility was that Benedict would move to the new sanctuary.

A Father Prior goes to meetings and Order of the Church gatherings, interacts with supporters of the church—gets about and is called upon to communicate. More importantly, perhaps, he is called upon to know how to take care of himself in the 'world out there.' Benedict, now in his early 30's, came to the monastic life as a very young man. A boy, I might say, factoring in his experiential limitations in the maturational process.

I asked Father Diamond if Don Benedict had he chosen the monastery life as a calling or as refuge. He told me that it was common for entrants to have been motivated by a combination of the two. He changed the subject abruptly. In any case, he said, my charge was to meet with Benedict once a week. I would assign readings from best works of world literature. The choices would be mine. We would then discuss the readings—and all other topics that were either germane or that either of us wanted to talk about. No restrictions on reading or topics discussed. None. "He needs to know as much as possible," Father Diamond said to me.

The eight or nine monks in the group on Mt. Equinox spoke only on Sundays, during a three-hour walk they had together. (A voluntary activity.) They were otherwise silent, singing notwithstanding. Two meals daily during summer, three during winter. They were served by "Brothers," men of lower standing who, essentially, were the workers in this vast complex. No newspapers, no *Time*, no televisions or radios were to be found up there—no contact or interest (supposedly) in the world at large. A strict and severe order. (Sometimes, visiting relatives smuggled in a rolled up magazine. *Playboy*? A terrible thought.)

The monks lived in individual, austere cells. They could tend a garden in a small plot outside one of the two doors in each cell. They had access to the monastery's library; most of the books I would bring for Benedict would not be found there.

Father Diamond, after our exchange of two hours and an additional hour spent on my responsibilities, said to me, "You would be a good monk, Harvey." I told him he might be right, but not in a silent order. He smiled. He then invited me to attend, as an observer, the five o'clock vespers. The monks convened and sang—chanted. I sat in the back of the sanctuary, separated from them by a partition of wooden slats that made viewing impossible. I heard them shuffle into their places, and soon they began their chanting. There was a strange feeling of peace that went through me—along with a sharp chill. The room was very cold. My teeth percussed to the singing. In my heightened state of spirituality, I prayed I wouldn't pee in my pants.

My first meeting with Benedict came the following week. Someone called the school to schedule it; if the time was satisfactory to me, I would just show up, stopping at the toll gate at the bottom of the mountain, having the guard give notice of my arrival, then driving up to my student with Dostoyevsky's *Crime and Punishment* on the seat beside me.

I was met by the hooded Benedict at the entrance and escorted to a small meeting room. After all the formalities had been taken care of, I told him to ask me a question that he might have been carrying around with him and wanted to hear an answer to. To my surprise (was *I* the naïve one?), it had to do with women. I sounded like Dr. Ruth. He was riveted. At the end of my lecture, he asked if I wanted to see his cell. "No one is allowed to do this, but you can be the exception," he told me. There had been an 'open house' for the locals, but that was before the monks moved in. Now the place was in lock-down.

I saw the spare and solitary room, the uncomfortable-looking bed, a chest of drawers, a table and a chair. I nodded and told him it was time for me to go. We would talk about the Russian novel I had brought to him next session. This time he nodded and reached out to shake my hand.

Don Benedict was—is—an extremely intelligent man. I hesitate to say brilliant, because there is some aspect to that word that indicates a 'shining'—and that does not work here. But his great intelligence had an analytical astuteness to it. What was right in front of him was immediately clear, but beyond that. . . . Well, perhaps that was lack of imagination or foresight or—experience. So I felt that it was my job to help him develop that ability.

We met regularly for two years. Kafka, Hemingway, James, Ibsen: he devoured them all and more. He had the time. His contributions to the talks became more assertive. More self-assured. He seemed to find fault in all of these writers. We had some spirited give and take, my 'giving' providing most of the spirit. His criticism was given with a cold determination. Almost a presumptuous arrogance. I tried not to be too aggressive. To restrain myself from saying things like, "How the hell would you know that, living up here in solitary?" I was never sure where this was going, but it would eventually be revealed, as all is.

I received a phone call at school. Don Benedict was being taken to the hospital. Nothing serious, one of the Brothers told me. Benedict had a problem with a deviated septum. He would have surgery early the next day. I visited him after school. He was sitting in his bed, alert, smiling, more animated than I had ever seen him. Nurses were fussing around him, propping pillows, bringing glasses containing soda and straws. Newspapers were at the foot of the bed. Life was good.

The next day I brought him two books. One was about Lincoln, my favorite. The other about Jefferson, his favorite. During my visit, the doctor came into the room. He told the patient that he could go home tomorrow or, if he wished, stay another day. Benedict looked at me, looked at the cute young nurse standing bedside and turned to the doctor. "I think I'd better stay another day."

At dinner that night, I said to Anita, "He's going to leave the monastery." She asked me what I was talking about. I told her Benedict was having too fine a time in the hospital. "After all the years up there on the mountain, he just had a whiff of the world in less rarified air. He liked it."

It took a while. Our meetings had become irregular. My feeling was that he did not see the original purpose as viable any longer; he did not project himself as a future Father Prior. He did not project himself as a future Father Anything. Two years later, after a phone call to me, he showed up at my door. We sat in the living room and I listened to him tell me of his leaving the order. I did not ask for rhymes or reasons.

He sought me out on a regular basis, calling ahead, then coming to the house. He seemed lost. Disoriented, at least. No wonder. What a dramatic change in his life—in his daily routine. He asked many questions and reached an eventual decision to go to visit relatives (his parents were no longer alive) in Pennsylvania.

Months later, he was at the door again, without forewarning, accompanied by a woman who was very evidently a few years his senior. She was "a cousin." They were considering marriage. Did he want my blessing? Well, my reaction, at least. "How nice," I said. They beamed.

I am not sure if the wedding ever took place. I don't think it did. I know he is married now, but I do not know the identity of the wife. At that time, he and his cousin left for upstate New York, where he was hired to do some work with computers. Computers! Had he hidden one under the bed in his cell? The University of Niagara was his new place in his new world. This guy must have been one quick study. Amazing.

I heard from him periodically. During one call he told me he had applied to Rome for release of his obligations, vows and the priesthood. During another call, he told me that, by special determination of the pope, his release had been granted.

Fast forward to 2002. Joe—that is his real name—discovered my whereabouts in North Carolina. He called to greet me, bring me up to date (married and living in Florida with a wife and dog) and, most importantly, to tell me he had written an autobiographical work. He asked if I would please read the manuscript and offer criticism and suggestion. "My friend told me it would definitely be a best seller," he said with great enthusiasm. I asked him if he had found a publisher. "No," he answered tersely.

"Fine, Joe. Send it along. I'll try to be helpful," I said.

It was at my door a few days later. Title: *I Used to be a Monk*. Best seller? Oh, my. From bad to worse. The story was dry and tedious. I offer no further literary criticism here, but I did send an e-mail to Joe letting him know my thoughts about the manuscript and what I believed he had to do to fix it. (If he could.) "Give the reader some insight into why you did what you did, what you were thinking, what reactions you had to circumstances, and so on," I wrote. "And, Joe, about that title: dump it. Think of something that would be more attractive to a potential reader. I offered a few suggestions off the top of my head. I did not believe them to be very good, but they were far superior to "I was a Monk."

I told him I would return the hard copy with the marginal comments I had made. He was grateful, he said. In 2005, a finished product came in the mail. The first thing I did was check out the publisher. It seemed to be a small 'vanity' press. The title was a definite improvement. (I withhold it, in deference to the Vatican witness protection program.) The presentation was greatly improved. It was not, in the vernacular, 'a page-turner,' and it did not become a "best seller." So what. He said what he had wanted to say. Most of it true.

The back cover tells the reader that Benedict, a.k.a. Joe, left the Carthusian order because of "unfortunate difficulties within that monastic community." Let it be. Joe inscribed the book to "My good friend and mentor." Not 'corruptor.'

The mentor, immediately after Joe had left Vermont, called the monastery and made an appointment with Father Diamond. Did I want to go to confession—to be told to say a 'Hail Mary' or two? A few 'Ave's?' I just wanted to express my sadness that I did not accomplish the task set out for me.

Father Diamond greeted me cordially. We sat. I offered what seemed to his ears to be an apology. "You are wrong in your thinking, Harvey," he said. "You did us a great service. If Father Benedict was inclined to leave the order, he would have either done so later, at an inappropriate time or have been very unhappy continuing to live a monastic life. Better that he—and we—discovered it now. He was not truly fit for the monastic life; you helped him to see that—and he is no longer a monk. All's well that ends well."

Was it an end for Father Diamond? Wasn't it a middle for me? But for Joe, who used to be a monk, it was certainly a new beginning.

2

Uber-Agent

Home from Tampa Bay, I enjoyed my dramatic schedule change. My new responsibilities were to the clients of Scott Boras, based on their needs—and my perception of a need they might have. The same rules applied: no presumptuous, intrusive behavior on my part. I may have believed that a player needed my intervention, but the player had to want it. The 'set-up' was easily achieved: Scott would be the vehicle to get the player to call me—if the player had not already initiated contact on his own.

The office had sent out letters to all the clients notifying players of my employment with the Scott Boras Corporation. The letter stated that "another resource" had been added to the staff. It provided my background. Most of Scott's players knew me or knew of me. Over the past fourteen years, while I was with Oakland, Florida and Tampa Bay I had greeted many of them around batting cages or in hotel lobbies. Many of the players, if not most, had read the books I had done on the mental game—often provided for them by Scott—and were aware of me through them.

My first major task was to travel to Florida and Arizona, where teams trained during spring training. I met with players for breakfast or dinner—or had brief 'hello-how-are-you?' sessions at the fields. Just to get in front of those who did not know me well and did not have any particular need to know me better at the moment.

During the season, I flew to see players whenever and wherever they wanted to get together to deal with their performance or personal issues. The phone was the instrument for follow-up. Multiple visits during the season were made with a number of players. The phone was usually in my ear when I was home, and often when I was on the road.

The winter months allowed for visits by players who felt a two-day get-together would be helpful. Five or six players came to our home each off-season. A few, in desperate need, came during the season; a few others came during the All-Star breaks.

Scott was happy with the arrangement, one he had envisioned years before. He told me early in our relationship that a job was waiting in his company when I was "tired of being in a uniform." Our initial meeting was encouraged by one of his clients, who happened to be the first of my "projects," so called by Oakland administrators. They defined a 'project' as a player who the organization valued and who was not achieving, according to that assessed value. Number one draft choice, Tim Belcher, told me I had to meet his agent, Scott Boras. "You two would get along fine; you're both assholes," he said with great affection.

He was right (about both?); we first got together for dinner on an off-day I had in Oakland. Over pasta (beer for me, water for Scott), we asked and answered questions about 'where we came from.' One of the attitudes that emerged and became clear to each of us was that the other had never learned to bow in order to be loved. Perhaps that is why 'Belch' said we were assholes. Others had said the same about me before. (A few Cubs minor league staff members who resented my existence, as I noted in a previous volume.) And, difficult as it is for me to accept second place, Scott is, according to all major media and executive sources in baseball (and fandom) Number One in the universe.

He is a difficult man. So am I. So are most people who do not have pleasing others as an approval agenda. Scott Boras is a man who came from humble origins. The son of a farmer, he was forced to work hard at something that was obligatory, not personally rewarding or satisfying. Milking cows, baling hay and driving farm equipment helped him develop a great respect for hard work.

I, personally, cannot fathom how he manages his current responsibilities. I am reminded of the guy on the Ed Sullivan show who would spin plates on sticks. He lined them up and gave them a nudge and went on down the line. As the first plate began to wobble, he ran back to give it another nudge and get it spinning again, repeating this activity before each plate fell and was irrevocably damaged. Energy, focus, determination. Skill. That's Scott. But the fellow on the Sullivan show did not need to deal with others who would interfere with his plates. He did not need to confront and negotiate and irritate and anger and assuage the fears of a feint-hearted client who would sell himself short rather than be perceived in the bad light of a resentful potential employer.

Dave Dombrowski, now the President and General Manager of the Detroit Tigers, told me, when we were both with the Marlins: "I hate Scott when I have to negotiate with him; I love him once we sign his player."

Dave knows that Scott will do anything to help his player reach the level of performance the team that signed him expected from him. Many times, while I was working during the summer for major league teams, Scott would ask me to fly into a city to meet with a player who needed a winter tune-up, so he could get his performance and/or self in order. Scott cares.

At the Italian restaurant in Oakland, during our first meeting, he said to me, "You look strange to me now that I see you out of uniform." My family had told me I looked strange to them *in* uniform. Perception is reality—to those who hold the perception. And that is why this uber-agent, now listed as one of the top ten most powerful men in sport, wealthy and intimidating, always opinionated and almost always right (Major League Baseball never comments on Boras-claims about increasing revenues, but Forbes magazine supports Scott's claims) is perceived as an arrogant, greedy bully.

He does not hold a gun to executives' heads; they are the ones who pay the money. They pay it because they think that Scott's players, most of them the elite in the game, are worth all the haggling, all—or close to—the figure Scott has determined for them. Business, plain and simple. But perceptions are not simple because they emanate from the complexities of the human mind and psyche.

The restaurant conversation moved to his faith ("a quiet Catholic"), his family (wife and three young children), and his concerns about being a good husband and father despite the great demands his work puts on his time and energy. He is not about greed; he is about need. The need to do his best. To satisfy that need, he drives himself relentlessly. And that can make for a difficult trip. It often has been, and I have tried to help him with the steering. Slowing him down does not seem to be an option.

The first client he asked me to deal with as a freelancer for his corporation was Greg Maddux. (Sandy Alderson had given me permission to work with individuals on other teams. ("Try not to deal with guys in the American League West," he told me.") Scott was there in Greg's motel room during my spring training visit in Mesa, Arizona. I had decided on an initial strategy beforehand. When I came into the room, the young Cubs pitcher was sitting on his bed playing Nintendo. Scott answered my knock on the door. I came in, said hello without a handshake—not wanting to disturb Greg's game—and pulled up a chair. I did not think the player would contribute much to this first conversation, given Scott's presence and the fascinating distraction of Nintendo, which Greg continued to play, until I asked for his undivided attention.

My major thrust was to scream at him that he had "no clue" how good he could be. I turned the intensity up from there, staying approximately forty-five minutes. After the tirade, I got up and left abruptly. Scott told me on the telephone that Greg's first words after I left were, "Who is that fucking madman?" Apparently Scott had not given him any introduction. On second thought, maybe he had.

Our relationship grew to be a close one. Greg asked me to call his brother, Mike, a pitcher with the Dodgers at the time (now the pitching coach of the Texas Rangers). I told Greg I don't call players; they have to call me. Mike did. So did Damon Berryhill, Greg's catcher and friend.

Scott's greatest concern was my fee. I low-balled myself, he told me. This after a few other interventions with his clients—and the same fee. "I feel guilty calling you," Scott said. "I hate that. I want you to work with my guys, but I don't feel good about asking." I had a simple solution: "Just pay me more," I said. He told me for the first of many times, "You're a shitty negotiator."

When he employed me full-time, we established a contract figure that was based on his understanding that the players would also pay me for my services. After some thought, I told him I believed this was not an effective way of utilizing me. Some players, already paying five percent of their salary for Scott's services, would be reluctant to pay out more money for mine. "They should all be able to pick up the phone and call. Period. And how does it sound for you to tell a guy he has to call me, because you think it's necessary, and he also has to pay me?"

The policy was immediately changed. My salary was raised; the players now had a resource that was part of the Scott Boras Corporation package. Everyone was happy, even the guy who had to bear the freight.

Scott and I have had our conflicts over the years, but they were resolved in a matter of days. Usually, in a matter of hours, after he had time to reflect. Am I suggesting that I was *always* right? The number of conflicts could be counted on one of Antonio Alfonseca's hands. (O.K. that needs explanation. A small, poor but irresistible joke. He was a Marlins pitcher with six fingers. After an especially effective inning pitched, he would come into the dugout and raise his hand to me. I would slap his palm with my right hand and the thumb of my left: a 'high-six.')

I was talking about conflict. Once, Scott called me and told me he did not want me to go to Arizona State University for a scheduled speaking engagement. He was angry at the baseball coach, Pat Murphy—also a difficult man. (Pat and I are very good friends.) I had been speaking at ASU for twelve years at that point. I was to fly there the following week. I will not repeat my diatribe to Scott. The general theme was that this was none of his business. He did not control my life. I was going to ASU. Did he know this? Of course. Had he known I would respond as I did? Almost certainly. But why not try? He tried. So, it has not been a matter of my rightness, but of his emotions getting in the way of his brain on a few issues. He never does this in his dealings with baseball executives, much to their chagrin. Because *they* do. Advantage, Boras.

The summer of 2006 was a rough one for me physically. As my pulmonary doctor, Roger Domby puts it, "You pushed the envelope too far." I have been told that I was "at war with my pathology"—with a lifetime asthmatic condition that affected my lungs significantly. My response to the first doctor who told me that was, "Who's winning?" Dr. Nash, here in Brevard, acknowledged that I was winning. He then said, "But that will not be the case forever." The end of forever came in 2006.

One of our players was suffering greatly. A prominent athlete playing in New York, he was on the edge of dysfunction. The very edge. Some thought he'd gone over. I was dealing with his issue and those of other players, flying in and out of cities, taking a small plane to a city in upstate New York, where an outstanding prospect was playing and in need. Then on to another city to see still another client. Next, back to New York.

All this had not been so unusual. This time, however, I was not well. I had managed to remain functional years before, working while having walking pneumonia, before coming home, collapsing, regenerating and going back to work. As predicted, that was not to be "the case forever." In his New York apartment, the Alex Rodriguez had to lean in close to me so he could hear the message I was gasping.

I went home and was admitted into the hospital the next day with a severe lung infection. Antibiotics, steroids and who-knows-what-else were sent coursing through my veins around the clock. For ten days. My recovery period at home was approximately six weeks. My immune system, said Dr. Domby, was shot. "You can't win that war any longer," he told me.

I asked him if he expected me to surrender. "No,' he said. "But you must declare a truce." He told me I could expect to be hospitalized once a year—"at least." Sure enough, I was back in Mission St. Joseph Hospital in Asheville in 2007. I thereafter made certain to 'behave'—to follow his edict: no flying, no contact with crowds or gatherings, no shaking hands, no hugging runny-nosed grandchildren, fetishistic hand washing—and so on. I told Anita I felt like Seinfeld's 'Bubble Boy.'

But I stayed out of the hospital in 2008—and to this point. (Not counting two hip replacements.) After my first episode in 2006, I called Scott and told him I would have to resign. He would have none of it. "Just do what you can do. First recover." I told him 'first' did not have a 'second.' I could no longer make spring training visits; I could no longer see players during the season—unless they came to me. He was unaffected. He said that Don Carman would increase his responsibilities.

Don Carman had pitched in the major leagues for ten years. He had been a Boras client and he became one of mine. We spent quite a bit of time together, and I will say this: given the difficulties of his childhood, this man became one of the great examples of mind over matter. What had so greatly mattered to him, he learned to control and master. He was intrigued by the process he had gone through and, after his playing days were over, he went to graduate school and earned a degree in sport psychology. I told Scott what he might not have known: I would not live forever. We hired Don as my 'assistant.' He is now his own very effective entity.

At first, Don dealt with the young minor league players. A good number of them have become major leaguers. And because of my travel restrictions, he has been running around, all over the country taking care of the needy. I sit at home on my backside in North Carolina—talking on the telephone and meeting with regular visitors who I pick up at the Asheville airport and take home for a two-day visit. That is what I do now.

Two years ago, I called Scott to tell him I wanted to cut my salary. He thought I was being ridiculous. "I told you you're a shitty negotiator," he said. I told him he had not felt right with our early financial arrangements, and I didn't feel right now. I presented him with the new figure. Silence betokens consent. Done deal. I *won* my case?

An article about me appeared in a 2008 issue of *Men's Journal*. In it, Scott told the writer that he was "fascinated by my initial conversations with Harvey, and I saw the results. Right then I knew I would attempt to hire Harvey. It took me a decade to get that to happen. (Fourteen years, actually.) He's tough to negotiate with." Say what?

I called Scott. "You were pleased with yourself, laying that 'tough to negotiate' shit on the writer," I said. "Very funny." He told me he was trying to make me look good.

However I look, however I feel, Scott Boras has treated me as well as I could ask any employer to treat me. We have forgiven each other for our few minor transgressions. The ones the people 'out there' hold him accountable for are fewer in number and lesser in significance than what is actually the case. Scott cares about his players' perceptions, not the image the public holds of him. The players know he cares; he knows he cares; I know the same.

In one of the many interviews he has been called upon to give, he told the interviewer that he intended to keep working until he is eighty. He is fifty-seven. At the same time, he tells me I have a "lifetime contract." Negotiation is imminent.

3

The Cage of Reality

Perspective is how one sees things—his experiences, his life, his daily situations. Needless to say, some people look and see one thing; others look and see something quite different. Positive perspectives, negative perspectives—and perspectives somewhere in between. Having just spent my time thinking about the perspective—and perceptions—many people have of Scott Boras, my mind has stuck with the biases, the cynicism, the fears—the many influences that shape people's view of their world. In my work, I have spent numerous hours dealing with players whose perspectives and realities were distorted.

I am reminded of the words of writer James Baldwin (he was required reading in my English class at De Witt Clinton High School in the Bronx; Baldwin was an alum.) "We take our shape . . . ," he wrote, "within and against the cage of reality bequeathed us at our birth; and yet it is precisely through our dependence on this reality that we are most endlessly betrayed." He could very well have been speaking about my clients. Of course, he was; he was speaking about all of us.

In an earlier volume, I wrote about a player who was anxious because his opponents on the other side of the field were "pros." I had to point out to the player that he, too, was a professional. How could he have been surprised to hear that? The answer rests on his personal "dependence" on whatever early experiences had shaped and "betrayed" him as an individual.

Some distorted realities can be very harmful; some are relatively harmless. I will provide one of each, from my early years, before discussing two encountered in my dealings with professional baseball players. The first story is an example of the power of brainwashing. As children, we are influenced by the words and actions of parents, teachers, clergymen, peers—and by experience. (Usually bedridden as a youth, I managed to avoid most of those. My father, the radio and books were the sources of my philosophical corpus.)

As we get older, the messages of politicians, advertisers and the media wash over our brains. The desire of others to coerce us, subtly and not-so-subtly, to have us think as they would have us think—to do what they would have us do—can add detail and color to the picture of our world, one that is being painted daily. We all end up believing many things that come from many sources.

To what extent are we aware of what has shaped our reality? To what degree do we allow for alternative views? Are we accepting of all we see and hear? Are we cynical? Is it possible to see clearly what is in front of us? What the hell *is* that in front of us? Are we capable of answering that one objectively? How many more questions of this type are rolling around in my head? Many.

The senior quarterback of my high school varsity football team lived in my neighborhood. I was a freshman and, having been kept soft by an over-protective mother and a bed-ridden childhood, I tended to idealize tough athletes. My goal was to be as tough as the toughest. (I did not believe I could ever be as athletic as any of them.) Joe Provenzano—a.k.a. Joe Pro—was my model. After he graduated, he did what we all knew he would do, though he never talked about it. He enlisted in the Marine Corps and was sent off to fight in the Korean 'Police Action.'

Before he left for boot camp, he told his pals that he would "cut off the nuts" of the first North Korean soldier he killed and "send them home to you guys in a box." That did not happen. What did happen was that Joe became a prisoner of war. The North Koreans were noted for their brain-washing techniques and, all too apparently, Joe was subjected to them. He was eventually released, and he returned home.

I remember seeing him on the streets. He was a shell of the person he had been. No self-assured bravado, no projection of strength—of certainty. Of awareness. My first thought was, "If this can happen to him, it can happen to anyone." The thoughts that followed were contemplative: about poor Joe—and about the power of forces outside ourselves, able to manipulate and shape our reality. Of our being seemingly helpless to fight against these forces.

Children, of course, are helpless. The forces that shape them may not be sinister, but they are powerful. And they are caged by them, as Baldwin puts it. They are betrayed to the extent that they fail to ever paint their own picture of their own world. Or fail to even attempt it. Children create the habit of seeking ways to satisfy their developing needs—or compensate for perceived inadequacies.

Melvin was an elementary school classmate. As infrequently as I went to school, I would walk the two short city blocks from my apartment house to P.S. 94. Melvin, a very quiet and non-threatening older boy would occasionally be heading to school at the same time. He would catch up with me (my pace would be no challenge for a slug) and walk at my side. He rarely spoke en route. But during one unguarded moment he revealed a fondness for animals. He expressed frustration that his mother was unwilling to allow cohabitation in their small apartment with any pet. "Not even a goddam Mexican Jellyfish," he said, surprising me with his language and great resentment.

However, Melvin's deep love for animals was not matched by a commensurate knowledge. He did not know a minnow from a Minotaur; an anal fin from a water hole. "Do *you* have any pets?" he asked. His pleading tone indicated to me the answer I had to provide. One I was all-too-willing to give. "Yes," I said tersely.

"What kind?"

"Dog."

That did it. During the school year and into the next, Melvin somehow managed to find his way next to me on the street on a more regular basis. Our conversation was exclusively on matters zoological. He asked after my dog, then about the cat I told him I had. Then a turtle (I really had one of those). Then a parrot. The reality of my menagerie grew in his mind as his appetite increased. Melvin's starving need was not satiated by the bare bones I had initially offered him, so I slowly added to what became a gourmand's menu.

This is out of control, I eventually thought. I felt terrible by then and tried, unsuccessfully to avoid him. He would find me. "Did you get a new pet?" With a death-wish finality, I told him I had been given a monkey. He was ecstatic. He cross-examined me whenever we met, until June, at which time Melvin, a year my senior, graduated from sixth grade and went on to a junior high school that it was my good fortune not to attend.

Twenty years later, while visiting my mother in the old neighborhood, I ran into Melvin, who was also there to see his widowed mother. We were walking in opposite directions and stopped abruptly when coming upon each other. I said his name, he said mine, certifying recognition. We shook hands and exchanged a few social platitudes. After this, I heard myself speak. More correctly, I heard a voice that sounded as if it were mine.

"Listen, Melvin, now that we're both adults, I want to tell you something. Remember those animals of mine?"

"Your pets?" He smiled. "Of course I remember."

Well," I said hesitantly, "They weren't real. They were just stories. You seemed to enjoy them so much. I . . . I mean there were no pets, you know."

"Don't be crazy," he said. "Of course there were. I saw them! I came up to your apartment and *saw* them. Remember?"

Melvin had never entered my apartment, but even had he . . . I pulled up my coat collar, but the chill's source was not external. We parted with a hand gesture, no further words spoken.

Melvin provided the ultimate reinforcement for something I 'knew' with a small 'k.' The capital 'K' was there now: People believe what they want to believe. What they *have* to believe. Many realities are painted for them and others they paint for themselves. (I think the motto of the college I attended is, "To each according to his need.")

The prevailing need of the professional players I work with is to be success-ful. (The negative expression of the goal, one used by too many of them is 'not to fail.') Whether the metaphor is a painted picture or a cage, it is provided for precocious young performers by parents, coaches, friends and fans. Many athletes suffer, as a result. They were so superior when they were young that all they had to do was show up and they would conquer their less gifted opponents. As they progressed—high school, college, pro-fessional baseball at the minor league level, advancement in the minors, reaching the major leagues—a reality awaited them that they have never before experienced: failure.

The duration of the difficulty they face depends on the resiliency of the individual, the ability to be rational, rather than emotional and the good luck to be supported, rather than chastised or abandoned. Most essential is the identification of strategies required to understand and alleviate the suffering: a plan for addressing the issue and solving it.

"Hold thoughts that are 'big'—about yourself, your life or your sport—at a distance from you," I tell players. I then hold a large sheet of paper in front of their eyes and ask them to describe what is in the room beyond the paper. After they say they cannot, I explain that the paper represents their baseball career. "A large object held too close to your face will block out the world beyond it. There is a world out beyond this paper, beyond baseball."

I typically tell a player he is a nice looking guy, he has a brain in his head, a good person with money in the bank that offers financial security (most of those I deal with do, indeed, fit this composite). I ask if they have a good marriage and most nod in affirmation. "You're a good son, a good hus-band, a good father. If a doctor told you would never play again, would you be all right?" Another affirmative nod. "You wouldn't kill yourself?" No.

"So we're not dealing with life or death here," I say, preliminary to get-ting at the specifics of the functional disorder on the field. Perspective first, as a foundation.

Walt Weiss was a favorite of mine. (I'll speak more of him in a later chap-ter.) A consistent and dependable infielder for the Oakland A's in the early

90's, he struggled with a sizable issue. I, too, was with Oakland at the time. Walt had been injured, and he thought Oakland's manager was losing his patience as he waited for his shortstop to recover. I will use Walt's words to make the point, words he gave to an interviewer more than ten years ago.

"I was really getting depressed," Weiss told the interviewer. "I mean, I hadn't played for close to a year. Harvey simply said to me, 'Okay, what's the worst case scenario here? What's the worst that can happen?' . . . He got me thinking not just about baseball, but about my life in general. He gave me the bigger picture, the larger view. . . . And once I did start to put things into proper perspective, I found that I could cope a lot better with the ups-and-downs of my career."

As always, easy to say; hard to do. Walt did it.

A few perspectives I heard over the years put me on my heels. One, in particular. A young minor league pitcher and I were standing behind the protective screen at second base during batting practice. I knew this boy to be 'wired tight.' I asked him if he had a girlfriend, and he answered that he did. "Do you think it's serious enough to lead to marriage?" I asked. He said it was.

What I said next I had never said before—or since. I cannot be certain what provoked me, but I think it was that, knowing the player, I wanted to test him, hoping that I would get a response that would allay whatever fears I had for the kid. I spoke: "What if I made you a deal? I would guarantee you will become a major league pitcher." A pause. "But I must kill your girlfriend before I make that guarantee."

It sounds even more absurd now than it did when I said it.

The next pause was an extended one. Tick, tick, tick. Then he spoke: "Jeez, Harv, that's a tough one." I am not inclined to repeat my lecture to him. Thank the Fates, he got to the big leagues, pitched a few years there—and married the girl who had dodged my mythical bullet.

Why does Barack Obama see the world as he does? Who painted Rush Limbaugh's world? Mother Teresa's? Lincoln's? Who built Hitler's cage?

I must devote my time to helping clients formulate their own personal answers to their own personal questions. I ration the energy I still have, using it to lend a hand as they struggle to pull off the bars of their cages and free themselves, so they may live in a world removed from the "reality bequeathed" them at birth—and beyond.

4

Words Written

Joseph Conrad believed that words are foes of reality. To someone who spends his life writing and talking about such matters as 'reality'—Conrad's statement could be disconcerting, to say the least. But while disagreeing with his generalization (I disagree with *almost* all generalizations), I can understand exactly how it can be appropriate when applied to specific situations. Many specific situations. Undaunted, I continue to write and speak.

The books I have written, without doubt, helped me to establish whatever level of credibility I reached with players. They discovered in *The Mental Game of Baseball, The Mental ABC's of Pitching* and *The Mental Keys to Hitting* that outstanding players before them had gone through similar difficulties. That there were elemental and easy-to-understand approaches for solving performance issues. No clinician in a white coat was required to 'fix' them.

They also learned that building a strong philosophical foundation came first, if they were to build a sturdy structure that could house 'the right stuff' of peak performance. There was nothing threatening in those books, so maybe they would not think the writer scary either.

That said, my responses to players who praised the book was a standard one—an honest caveat: "The tool is only as good as the worker." I told them deeds were the payoff. The words were just instruments—means to their desired ends.

F.P. Santangelo was a young player with the Montreal Expos in 1996. After a spring training game, he asked his teammate, Wally Whitehurst, to introduce him to me. Wally and I had been together with Oakland. In fact, he was one of the Instructional League visitors to our home in Prescott, "the one with the gorgeous eyes," as Anita still identifies him. (He was the one she put to work with a wheelbarrow and shovel.)

F.P. came out of the locker room holding a copy of *The Mental Game of Baseball*. He shook my hand then offered me the book. One could say it had the appearance of extreme stress—of great use. Or one could say the player's dog used it as a push-pull toy. What can be said with certainty is that the pages were worn, torn, marked with highlighting, underlining and marginal notes. It actually reminded me of a cookbook I saw my mother use regularly when I was a child. My immediate response was to offer to send him a new one—in mint condition.

F.P. was startled. "Are you kidding?" As if mine had been an outrageous suggestion. "I know exactly where everything is in this book," he said. "I just wanted to show you how valuable it is to me."

"I see you've read it and written in it—referred to it often," I said. "But I want to know if you applied any of it to your game." He tilted his head and said, "Are you kidding?" A favorite question of his, I suspect. After I nodded to let him know I understood rhetorical questions, he moved off, leaving Wally and me standing there shrugging shoulders at each other.

F.P. finished fourth in the National League Rookie of the Year voting that year. His talent was modest, but he extracted every bit of it from his limited body—by utilizing his mental tools. F.P. played almost every defensive position on the field and also became an occasional designated hitter. He was the prototype 'blue collar player:' dirty uniform after each game, in the top ten for years in the category of "hit by pitch" and he played the game hard—the right way. Because he was a switch-hitter, he was able to earn the distinction of being hit by pitches from both sides of the plate in the same game. F.P. was a doer. My kind of reader.

The integration of information into behavior is what concerns me greatly. It is a theme I harp on—to the annoyance, I am sure—of those who have heard it enough to have it qualify as an *ad nauseum* theme. But I persist.

Sections of self-help books can be found in any bookstore and writers find new ways of saying the same things most have said before them. Readers browse the shelves, pick a *Chicken Soup for the Feint of Heart* from the stacks, flip through and say to themselves, "Yes, this is what I need." They purchase the book, take it home, read it—perhaps—and go on behaving in the same chicken-shit way as in the past. They do not change. These are the same people who made New Year's resolutions—vows to themselves—and broke them (as statistics show) after two months, tops, or two weeks, more likely. Great book though. And a picture taken of their shelves will look like a Barnes & Noble ad. Resulting in what? A need for more shelves?

F. P. Santangelo's major league career was limited; a number of other exemplary readers of the books on the mental approach have had greater talent and were therefore able to apply principles to performance with greater success. Clients of mine who were most notable in this regard include Greg Maddux, who will be a Hall-of-Famer, Roy Halladay, who, if he stays healthy, has a chance to enter those hallowed halls, and Jamie Moyer, who at age forty-eight, is still pitching in the big leagues. All of the pitchers, conscientious readers of the books, especially *The Mental ABC's of Pitching*, have what I call the 'insistent wills' to transfer written principle into behavioral consistency. I admire them all. And many others, though these three pitchers have separated themselves from the others. (When Halladay finishes a reading of the book, he starts all over again, he told me. I told him to find some other books to read.)

Al Leiter was also dedicated to intense application and strong advocacy. I told him he acted as if he were my agent. He introduced to me players who he felt had a need and introduced the book to every player who would listen, since, he said, "They *all* have a need to read that stuff."

An authentic literary agent called me from New York a few years ago. A professional of some repute (I made a couple of calls to check on him), he asked if he could come to Carolina to visit me. "To what end?" the ever-skeptical me asked. "Well," he began, hesitatingly, "I think you should write a book; I have an idea." A good number ('bad number' would be a more appropriate description) of people call me with ideas that hover over ridiculous and non-sublime creative territories. Writing a book may sound clear-cut and tangible, but the subject is always my concern.

Before he addressed that concern, he tried to distract me with grandiose talk of "a six-figure advance" he said he could get for me. That remark created a seven-figure suspicion on my part. "Get to the real point," I said. What's the subject of the book?"

"That's what I want to discuss with you when I come to Carolina," he answered, without answering. I still search the recesses of my memory, seeking a clue that will help me discover why I consented to a visit. The reason is yet to be revealed; the consent was given. He would fly from New York the following week to spend a day with me.

A large man, in size and, according to the vitae he showed me, in professional standing, David looked uncomfortable as he sat in a comfortable chair in my home office. (Had *he* made a few calls also?) After philosophical foreplay, he engaged himself with the main event: the idea. I expected little, and I got less. Essentially, he was open to any idea *I* had—any topic— that would be treated between the covers of what amounted to another self-help book. My response came before he had swallowed the final word of the idea's death sentence.

"I have no intention of adding to the manure pile." His calm demeanor led me to believe he had known exactly what my response would be. He was prepared for that, but he did not seem to be prepared to debate the merits of his point of view and the demerits of mine. Instead, he tried to convince me with 'arguments' based on money and the needs of the masses. An appeaser feeding the crocodile, as Churchill put it, hoping it would eat him last.

I railed on about books that accomplish nothing and my unwillingness to pursue his project. The day dragged on for both of us. I would wager that he could not now remember anything I said, aside from "No." I certainly remember nothing but his 'yeses.' Shortly before he left, he presented a creative compromise: "How about you telling me a topic you're interested in that might be able to fit what I had in mind?" he said.

The knee-jerk, "No." Then (because he said nothing?), I had a thought. "Well, the topic of 'courage'—in the context of personal inter-action, interests me. The absence of it, actually. I'm interested in my prevailing view that people, based on my experience, lack the courage of their conviction; the self-discipline to do what they know is the right thing to do. The obstacles and so on."

He beamed. "That'll work," he said, ever the agent of optimism, the digitalis of failure.

I said I would give the idea some thought and give him a call in a few days. When the call was made, David said he was happy to hear from me, and happier still that I would follow procedures and practices of the trade and submit a proposal and couple of chapters. This I did.

Two weeks later I received a call from the literary editor in his office, a young woman who told me she liked what I had written. "But you have to dumb it down," she said. I asked her what the hell she was talking about. She answered that it sounded like a college text book. I asked if she had read any of the stuff I wrote about in the baseball books. She said she had. I asked what she thought of them. She said she liked them. I told her that what I had just submitted was exactly the same style, language, syntax and vocabulary. She said, "Maybe so, but you still have to dumb it down."

So I worked on the chapters. "Dumb enough?" I asked her in a note that accompanied the revised pages. "No," she said during our next phone conversation. I asked her how old she was. Taken aback, she answered. "Twenty three, but please don't tell anyone." The only thing I told anyone was that this project was terminated. I think I used a dumber word than 'terminated.'

I still am interested enough in the topic of courage; I talk with clients about the subject on a regular basis. I'll discuss it in a later chapter—in a moderately literate fashion, I hope.

Instead of writing the book I was asked to write, I wrote a book for coaches. Actually, a good number of people had asked me to pursue that project. As one coach said to me, "You write all that stuff for players, but coaches could use some help dealing with the mental game." The result was *Coaching the Mental Game.*

I do not rue the day when I started writing books telling people what to think, how and when to think it—all the while wondering whether these words would translate into behavior. But I must say it was more fun, when living and teaching in Vermont, to knock off a newspaper column or feature story that, I hoped, could just entertain or inform.

I produced a satirical piece about the State Legislature cutting off free coffee in the name of fiscal responsibility. (They re-instated the policy after my article 'pointed out'—among other things—that state representatives 'no longer had a reason to meet and speak with each other each morning, so fewer bills were developed or discussed.')

Another satire appeared, in the form of a dialogue between the Governor and his aide. The theme of their discussion was the possible implementation of a crash program to get Miss Vermont to win the Miss America Pageant, thereby helping the Governor to get re-elected. During the conversation, the Governor bemoaned the fact that a Vermont girl had never done any better than winning Miss Congeniality. (This was a fact.) But how could that change? This year's Miss Vermont played the violin, of all things. (Another fact.) The two actors in this farce batted around ways to gain the crown for our Vermont girl. It was an imperative, if the Governor was to be assured of re-election. A feather in his coonskin cap. My paper's owner and publisher wrote an irate editorial the next day blasting the Governor. The old guy thought my writing was reportorial rather than satirical. A disclaimer from my editor appeared the following day, telling readers my article "was not true."

Stories appeared in the in the pages of the *Rutland Herald* about Vermont roads, the Vermont Transit bus line, a senator's wife and the Susan B. Anthony dollar (a failure confused with a quarter because of its size—and given life by the Secretary of the Treasury—a Vermonter, who, I wrote, had 'hoodwinked' the so-called sophisticates in our grand country). Other stories about a state Supreme Court justice and a local rural mailman were written. All with no expectations on my part for the readers, except, perhaps, to have them enjoy the reading as much as I enjoyed the writing.

I did not have to shout, as I later did to players. "You don't read these books so you can know; you read them so you can *do!*"

5

Words Spoken

A tangential activity developed from my professional work on baseball fields and between book covers. People who represented a variety of groups invited me to speak at meetings and conventions. It was like being at the front of a classroom again. I enjoyed myself, trying to vary my experiences, accepting those offers that were 'different' from previous ones.

The first invitation came early in my baseball years. A group of businessmen had gathered at the same hotel I was staying at in Scottsdale during my third Instructional League with Oakland.

A man knocked on the door of my room one evening. I realize as I write this that he seems young in my memory's eye, but he had undoubtedly logged as many years as I had by then: close to fifty. He told me of his banking group's interest in having me speak. "Can you fire something up for the night after next?" he asked. He wanted the group's collective psyche to be "fired up." To use his exact term of clarification, one that is abhorrent to me, he wanted me to deliver "a motivational speech."

I was happy to supplement my income but not so indiscriminate that I accepted the assignment without reservations. I did not express these reservations to him, but I was determined not to fill the room with bullshit. Nor did I want a room full of head-nodding suits. I wanted to provoke action going forward, not inspiration for people who sat on their status quo asses.

I enlisted the aid of one of the bellman, a young fellow I had gotten to know well. (He was getting his pilot's license and needed to log hours, so he was happy to fly me home to Prescott on weekends—a forty-minute flight. Anita waited at the little airport wringing her hands, thinking me crazy—again.) I told Billy to stay inside the small convention room during my talk, because I wanted him to turn the little knob on the shut double doors. The exit doors were opened by pushing out from the room and could only be locked from the inside.

Done.

I launched into a Knute Rockne pep talk, 'motivating' the vests off these sports enthusiasts with stories of determination and achievement and more. The 'more' part is best described by the words of Mark Twain: "Truth is mighty and will prevail. . . . Except that it ain't so." Ah, but they lapped it up the way Melvin had lapped up the water in my imaginary dog's bowl. I do not mean to imply that I was telling tall tales. I mean to absolutely *confess* to it. But woven into the fabric of the presentation were threads of important truths. Whatever the case, the audience seemed to receive it well.

After forty-five minutes, I gave them the final word. I thanked them and said in my best locker-room style, "Now go out there into the world and kick some ass!" They jumped from their seats and poured into and up the aisles. And hit the immovable doors. Literally. But for these actors' outfits, the scene could have come from a Keystone Kops film. The doors were locked, of course, and the hard chargers banged into them, then each other, and then—some of them fell in a pile on the floor. The mood I had created did go out the doors—under the cracks or through, exiting like a phantasm. The men were stunned.

I then shouted out: "Everyone!—Get back to your seats!—I forgot to tell you something!" They moved as if in a dream—or in a death march—and returned to their seats. The room was eerily quiet. I spoke in a modified, somber tone. "What I forgot to tell you is this: For every four of you who went charging up the aisle, only one of you—*one!*—will do what we were talking about here today. Who will that one be?"

I then disappeared, going out stage left, never to see them again. (I already had my check.)

That scenario was never developed again. It was enough to tell the story in the many presentations I made in the future. The theme was the always the same: After all is said, what is done? Samuel Butler had gotten it right about words: ". . . nothing so useless unless when in actual use." I believed it then, I know it now.

An insurance agent called me during a Prescott winter, asking if I would speak to a small group of agents he managed. The topic he wanted treated was "rejection." I understood, having rejected many insurance agents in the past. (Anita's childhood friend finally cracked the ice. He had her on his side, and he represented Northwest Mutual, a reliable outfit, I thought.)

After I had spoken my words about rejection—the why's and what-to-do's—the manager came up to me, thanked me and made another request. He wanted me to "work with (him)" because he had a hard time speaking in front of this group that met regularly. "You look cool and calm up there," he said. "When I'm speaking, my palms are wet, my arm pits are sweaty, my mouth is dry, my heart is thumping in my chest."

I told him I wanted to watch him before I agreed. The next week I did. After he had finished and the others left, Joel came to the back of the room, where I had seated myself. "See what I mean?" he said.

I said, "You mean about your palms and pits and so on?"

"Yes," he answered.

I told him that I couldn't see all those manifestations of nerves. "What I did see is that you were organized, you presented your points orderly and clearly and, though you're not a Greek orator, you're certainly effective enough. The audience has no idea about your nerves. So that is the highest praise I can give. I ask my shaky players to behave appropriately in spite of their feelings. You did that. You don't need me."

Tim Belcher, the pitcher who had introduced me to Scott Boras, now had another pal he thought did need me. He wanted me to get together with his former college coach. I told him he ought to run a dating service. He wasn't even listening. "He just got the job at Southern Illinois; he's replacing Itchy Jones (a local legend) and I think he could use your help." (His former coaching assignment was the small Ohio school Belcher had attended.)

Off I went to Southern Illinois, spending three days speaking with staff, individual players and groups. My presentations were, apparently, aggressive. I had determined that was what was needed, because the coach was a gentleman—too restrained, I thought, and soft in manner. I probably overcompensated. This thought was confirmed on my last day there.

The talk had just about ended. I would close with my redundant theme: *doing* what you know. I asked the audience, "What are the two words that I hear most in my job?"

Hands were raised in the small auditorium. I pointed at a young man at the back. He gave his answer: "Fuck you." The other players—even the mild-mannered coach—went bonkers. I smiled and stood, waiting. When everyone quieted down, I spoke. "*That* is number two," I said. "Number one is 'I know.'" I explained as I plodded through my finish line, but this kid had won the day, no doubt. Still, it was a story I could use forever. And have.

I was invited to speak at a considerable number of schools. Most invitations were, understandably, extended by baseball coaches (and a few women's softball coaches). The first university I spoke at was right there in the Scottsdale area: Tempe, where Arizona State University is located. Grady Fuson, now running the minor league and scouting systems of the San Diego Padres, was then an Oakland scout. We had become close as a result of frequent professional associations—and an involvement in a very personal situation he asked me to help him with.

Grady's uncle was an ASU icon. The baseball facility is now named after him. He died of cancer in 1994, after coaching there for twenty-three years and winning two national championships. Grady's uncle had also gained the reputation of being a sarcastic, cynical and gruff man. This reputation was based on accurate assessment. Jim Brock was, people said, a very difficult man. (His wife had no trouble putting him in harness, I was to find out. And he became close to docile in his dealings with me.)

Jim reluctantly 'allowed' me to come to Tempe to speak to his team. (This less-than-enthusiastic accepting term used when he gave Grady the go-ahead.) Grady had told him it was "a must." So I went, I saw, I spoke. As it turned out, I conquered the irascible Jim Brock. When my presentation was completed, he came up to me and said, without a handshake or a smile, ""You're the first psychologist I ever met who isn't a pussy."

"What can I say after such high praise?" I offered.

"You don't have to say a damn thing. Just come with me to dinner." And for six years, that was the venue: talk to his players followed by dinner with Jim at his favorite local steak house. (After the first two years, his wife joined us.)

Jim's replacement, Pat Murphy, was the third coach in the history of the school's program. (Bobby Winkles was the first.) My initial meeting with Murph took place when he was coaching Notre Dame. He had me speak to his team during the team's spring trip to Scottsdale. Murph had a reputation—much of it deserved—that was more dramatically negative than Brock's.

We spent considerable time together during ensuing years. His growth as a man and a coach went well beyond the time we spent together. In other words, this guy, coming out of a difficult childhood circumstance, worked conscientiously, consistently and effectively on self-development. Many 'out there' fail to acknowledge the change. Is it easier to remember what you didn't like about a guy than what you did like? Aside from my personal relationship with him, Murph had me intensify my involvement with the Sun Devils program.

That involvement ended after seventeen years, because of my health. Murph has come to visit me in North Carolina, and we still talk regularly on the phone. (My final address to one of his teams was a conference-call question & answer session.)

Aside from the many visits to schools throughout the country, I occasionally spoke to corporate groups, large and small. My favorite story about a visit of this type began with Jeff Musselman. Jeff was a talented left-handed pitcher with the Toronto Blue Jays. He was not living up to his potential, and the Jays lost patience with him. They did not know he was battling an alcohol problem. I learned about it when he was traded to Oakland. He and I spent much time together. He put himself into the AA program and made great strides off and on the field, pitching for the A's Triple-A team in Tacoma.

Jeff, in my estimation, would have become a very successful major league performer. A Scott Boras client at the time, he was weeks away from being recalled by the big team, when he had an episode that literally brought him to his knees outside his Tacoma apartment. It was related to a complicated heart malfunction, one that he again had to deal with two years ago. He is now fine and has, for some years, been Vice-President of the Boras Corporation. He actually administers to the business and staff at the corporate headquarters in Newport Beach, California. A Harvard graduate, Jeff is highly intelligent—and sensible. His sufferings have made him even smarter—because he survived them.

While he was working out at the local gym one day in the mid-1990's, an acquaintance approached him. This fellow worked for Fluor-Daniel, a conglomerate involved in large construction projects worldwide. He told Jeff he was responsible for getting a speaker for the upcoming corporate convention to be held in Houston two months from that day. He said he was having a hard time. "I need someone who is very confrontational," he said. "The most aggressive guy you know. Borderline obnoxious, if possible."

As Jeff continued this report, he told me his words for the needy searcher were simply, "I have just the guy for you."

I subsequently spoke on the phone with the corporate officer in charge of the program. He told me that, while the company was doing very well, he "sensed some complacency festering below the surface of the field managers' daily approach. "They need to be provoked," he said. "I don't care how you do it, but you have to let them know that self-satisfaction is unacceptable." This, he wanted from me while all was right with the managers' world? Lotsa luck, I said to myself.

But I was determined to fulfill my responsibility. While I was, I thought, successfully doing just that, many in the audience did not hear it that way. Sitting at round tables in a very large dining room, those who would have their backs to me turned their chairs to face me. As the talk got into the confrontation message, many turned the chairs back to their original positions. Others did not bother; they just got up and walked out. I was wowing them?

I wowed the boss, apparently. He came up to me after the audience's tepid response of applause that sounded as if they were pounding a pillow. "That was exactly what I wanted!" he said excitedly. "You just made me half-a-million. (The wonderful world of corporate bonuses.) That was what they had to hear, whether they liked it or not."

I told him it was clear to me that many did not. "The more of them that floated on you, the better," he answered. "The more likely the message will get them off their asses." (I had used a story in my talk that my father had told me about workers and ass-rising.) My compensation was quite acceptable to me, though a bit distant from this man's half-million.

I did not think myself to be a barker outside a circus tent, but I was certainly tried to be forceful in my delivery. OK, aggressive—and, to my mind, honest. (An Oakland player, Brain Graham, described me in a newspaper interview as being "brutally honest.")

But I could be quite mellow when the circumstance allowed for such a gentle spirit. One example to validate that claim is a talk I gave to faculty members of the pharmacology department at St. John's University. My topic was "The Pharmacist as Healer." I harkened back to 'the good old days,' when neighborhood drug store proprietors were all called 'Doc.'

During my Bronx boyhood, the Doc located on the corner of Putnam Place and Gun Hill Road extracted splinters from my hands and legs, took foreign bodies out of my eyes, took my temperature (orally, thank you)—and tied with twine mysterious boxes wrapped in green paper. These packages would be delivered to one of my two older sisters. (I questioned a boy who lived in my apartment house; he had an older sister. "It's Kotex, stupid," he told me. What's that? I asked myself, not daring to reveal my further stupidity.)

I told the St. John's men and women that now, the pharmacist stands behind a partition on an elevated platform and dispenses prescriptions, most often handed to the customer—the patient," I added—by some clerk. No Doc; no personal contact. I offered opinions about how this situation, so unfortunate in my view, could be remedied to some degree, though never to the extent I would wish.

A fellow sport psychologist who lived nearby had asked me if he could attend the session. After it was completed, and I had 'mixed' with faculty members, he told me that he hadn't known I could speak that way. I paraphrased the poet, Matthew Arnold: "Calm isn't my crown, though calm is well," I said. He was already headed for the snack table.

After each of us had managed a cuppa and a mini-sandwich, we went downstairs for another presentation of mine. My pharmacological host had asked if I could "spend a few minutes with our baseball players." I was not calm down there.

Taped to the base of my computer stand are the words of Thomas Paine: "Moderation in temperament is a virtue; moderation in principle is a vice." One out of two ain't bad?

6

Predilections

It is folly to expect people to do what is reasonably expected of them. So when our expectations of others are met—or exceeded—our view of these people can be swayed to an extreme. Any teacher who claims never to have had favorite students—'pets'—is either lying or has no real regard for people. Having taught for twenty-seven years, I am able to draw from a vast roster of students. I remember well the favorites and—all-too-well—their counterparts.

For the past twenty-six years, I have been dealing with professional athletes, who also qualify as students: quick learners, slow learners and non-learners. But baseball players have an expectation beyond the computing of information by their brains. They must *apply* the learning in a rather immediate sense. That application—performance—is the basis for judgment of their relative merits. A very good player, a decent player, a poor player.

A number of other factors determine the manner in which a player projects himself. Just as a student's personality can be appealing or off-putting for a teacher, so too can an athlete's. What most influences the way coaches, managers and front office personnel feel about a player—aside from his talent—is usually called 'attitude.' It is often, and inaccurately, called 'make-up.' I will not get into the distinctions here, though there are a good number of them.

Animal pets can please their owners by being cute and compliant. Favorite players need only be cooperative, coachable, hard-working, responsible, unselfish, self-sacrificing, helpful to teammates, dependable, productive in crucial situations and relentless in the pursuit of excellence. They do all the right things on and off the field. What's not to like about such guys?

A fair number of players exhibit a fair number of these qualities. Few exhibit all. That is not to say that those who fall short of scoring at the very top of the complete list are not valuable team assets. They assuredly are, but they do not qualify as favorites.

As for others who fall lower on the list, let it be said that, though a mother may appreciate a son's sullen brilliance, teachers and coaches only appreciate the brilliance. I, myself, was not a bad person when the fine woman who was my high school geometry teacher wrote about me in the comment section of my report card: "Highly obnoxious." She still gave me a grade of 92.

I was neither brilliant nor sullen, but the point should be clear. Pains in the ass do not win favor with the ass-owners. An obnoxious attitude or antic gets in the way of personal relationships. It precludes the possibility. So, thinking back, I can recall many players who I held in high regard, many players who I respected greatly, many players who would score high on every judge's list. I can also remember vividly the few pains-in-the-ass—as well as a couple who were, I thought, 'bad guys.' I can name few who qualify as 'pets'—people with whom I connected, for a variety of reasons, in a very special way.

Before I pursue those specific memories, I must acknowledge the problem with the term 'pet.' It starts with the inference that certain favored individuals are treated differently. The real problem is not where the inference starts, but where it *ends*: a conclusion being drawn that non-favorites are treated unfairly, at best, poorly, at worst.

If that truly is the case, the problem is not a semantic one but a behavioral one. My treatment of each individual should be pragmatic and insightful, in spite—or because—of a player's distinct personality difference. But do not ask me to go out and have a beer with some of them. For me, the litmus test of fairness has not been how I treated individuals personally, but how I treated them professionally.

My standard for behavior has not changed from player to player; my approach has. I was given an early lesson by my father, an avid and astute betting man who spent much time analyzing racing forms and thoroughbreds up close. "People are like horses, kid," he started. (To my disappointment, this was to be a lesson in human, not equine, psychology.) "Some, all you gotta do is hand-ride 'em. They'll take care of business by themselves. Some you gotta show the whip to. Make sure they pay attention to business. The rest you gotta beat the shit out of."

What I have managed to learn for myself over the years, is that the most powerful motivation is self-motivation. The whip—shown or applied—works. But it had better be a short race. A lifetime is a long distance, and the best people take whatever lessons they have been subjected to and propel themselves toward the distant finish line with enthusiasm, energy and focus.

That should bring my point of view out into open view. So down the stretch I now come to catch up with those memories waiting for me in the form of pets. Chronology provides order to my recollections, so the players are presented as I met them in time.

Walt Weiss was the player in Pocatello, Idaho, who was introduced to me as I ranted and raved at a team of rookie league players, the subject of my talk being the bullying treatment a couple of North American players (one was Canadian) were dishing out to the predominant majority of Latinos on the team and the consequences should this harassment continue. Walt's whispered wonderment to the only other Caucasian teammate—'*This* is our psychologist?'—put him at some perceptual distance from me that day. We closed the gap quickly.

He was in the same sport psychology class as my daughter, Melissa, when they were students at the University of North Carolina at Chapel Hill. He had not heard a presentation in his class that approximated my Pocatello act. We had a good laugh about his first impression.

In 1988, Walt won the Rookie-of-the-Year Award. His steady, dependable approach to the game won him the reputation as a model of consistency. He had worked hard at it, making infield practice mentally meaningful to the fullest extent possible. Too many infielders treat fungo drills in a perfunctory fashion. Not Walt.

All this aside, he and I just 'hit it off.' (We both were avid followers of Tar Heel basketball, of course.) I noted in an earlier chapter the difficult times he went through while we were together in Oakland. He was not, we both thought, given the proper consideration and respect he deserved after having recovered from an injury. My open support of him solidified our relationship.

Walt does not have the facial contours of a movie star. Some players thought what they called his "drop-jaw' indicated an uncertainty or confusion about what was going on around him. The reality belied the appearance. His look was someone else's 'thinking cap.' Walt either knew what was going on or was in the process of discovery.

Another Oakland player came up to me in the locker room one day. He was aware of the relationship I had with Walt. "Harv," said the player, "Have you seen the woman Walter's been hangin' with?" I had not. The player continued: "He's over his skis, man." I too had been so identified by some of players. One is over his skis when, as a not particularly attractive person, he has somehow won the heart of a *very* attractive woman.

Always concerned, and justifiably so, given past experience with other players, I thought of the worst scenario, so as to identify what *might* be a problem. From the low minor leagues and on up the ladder of status, both professional and financial, young athletes I dealt with have been approached by groupies, gold-diggers, free-loaders and the like—identified because their goal is to latch on to a potential meal-ticket. It is a sad truth that one can bear witness to just walking to the team bus after a game in, say, Walla Walla, Washington.

In this regard, I can think the worst though hoping for the best. But I must help protect a player from his innocence when and if possible.

"Hey, Walter," I greeted him in the clubhouse. "I hear you have a lovely lady on your arm these days."

As I suggested, Walt gets it. He knew the exact location of my concerns: his lady's motives and agenda. He was quick to speak. "When we first got together, she didn't even know I was a ballplayer." He wore the grin of a canary that just swallowed the cat. We shared another laugh, two skiers who had successfully negotiated what could have been a slippery slope. Walt, his lady—his wife—and children happily reside in Colorado, where he is an infield instructor in the Rockies organization.

We were together again after Walt was traded to the Marlins. It was there that the highest praise a 'baseball guy' could ever wish for was given me by Walt. A number of us were in the shower after a Marlins game. A young pitcher, knowing of Walt's impending free agency, said to him, "What team would you most want to play for?"

Walt nodded in my direction. "Any team he's with." That was a counter-vailing force against any of the bad days I had.

Other A's players come close: Terry Steinbach, Bob Welsh, Dave Stewart—and a host of minor league players who never became major leaguers because of a surfeit of talent. Some made it there but did not last long. What drew me close to them was their persona, not their talent—or lack of.

Jim Abbott is, like me, a bibliophile, so that bound us together immediately. He would ask for book suggestions frequently and share his critiques. Most people are aware of the fact that Jim has no right hand. Despite winning the prestigious Sullivan Award for his pitching at the University of Michigan, and despite propelling himself right into the major leagues, Jim could look at these achievements in a dark shadow of self-perception rather than in the rays of light emanating from all who admired the person and his achievements.

When Jim first came out to see me in Arizona, I picked him up at the airport in Phoenix. We stopped en route to Prescott for a quick lunch-time bowl of chili. As we were getting back into the car he said, "You've made me talk more about my hand in forty-five minutes than I have in my entire life."

"Isn't that why you're here?" I asked.

Nowadays, Jim is open and candid about the prerequisites for thinking right and living right. One is the rejection of the term 'handicapped.' He speaks to many groups of physically challenged young people who need and heed his message, delivered with his winning personality, his honesty and his empathy.

Jeff Conine and Greg Colbrunn remain pals of mine. Greg has visited me in North Carolina a number of times. Anita and I dined with him and his wife, Erika, during their vacation visit to Asheville and the Biltmore House.

Jeff is a phone and e-mail friend. He and Greg played the game right and live their lives joyfully and responsibly. When the Marlins had an off-day in Philadelphia, Jeff—aka 'Niner'—would hire a limo, and the three of us, accompanied by Rick Slate, the strength and conditioning coach, would have an all-nighter at the gambling tables in Atlantic City. Obviously, my kind of guys.

Charles Johnson was the Marlins catcher while I was there. His quiet, un-assuming manner belied the intense competitive fire that burned within. He was soft on others while being very hard on himself. A Boras client, Charles was playing for Tampa Bay years after I had left that team. He wanted to leave also. His struggles had provoked thoughts of quitting. Though we spoke on the phone, I had not seen him in years. I was con-vinced he was making a poor decision, so I hopped on a plane to visit him in Florida. Charles picked me up at the airport. I slid into my seat; we shook hands.

Charles then shook his head. "Harv, man, you're still doing this shit." Not spoken as a question but as an expression of wonder. ('Here is this old guy still doing his shit, and I want to quit doing mine.') We spent the day together, joined by his wife, Rhonda. Charles was double-teamed. He returned to the Devil Rays and played on.

Our discussion had not centered on what he wanted to do but, rather, his motive for doing it. Once clarity was achieved, Charles re-established his former attitude—his old self. The one that I so valued—as did Rhonda. As did Charles himself.

I could write a book about Al Leiter. Suffice to say, he is unique. A good number of people have labeled him "different." That is easily determined. But those who know him well use the term "special." Our relationship endures: visits, phone calls, e-mails—and the on-going Leiter recommen-dations that people call me for a multitude of reasons. He could qualify as my agent—and friend. He has visited me at every house Anita and I have lived in during our 'baseball years.' An impromptu visit in 2009, provoked Anita, who had not seen him in ten years, to say, "Isn't he cute? And he's forty-three, the same age as Dan." I told her there are many people who are the same age as Dan, and that forty-three-year old men aren't "cute." She ignored me: her typically appropriate response to my boorishness.

A few on-field staff members and front office personnel are among the limited number I would have a predilection to call 'favorites.' Geography does not change our relationships; we find a way to stay in contact.

Extended thought leads me to recollections of some players with whom I failed to establish a secure connection. Some failed by design, others because of fateful circumstance. Two particular stories I recall clearly. A resentful, bitter and angry young outfielder, who the A's acquired in a trade with the Angels for a veteran pitcher, established himself as a thorn in the collective backside of minor league instructors. A second round draft choice, he had been angered by the organization that chose him, nurtured him—and then, in his mind, betrayed him. He took his anger out on the Oakland staff. He and I spent time together and he listened politely but without observable effect. He rose to the Double-A level, perhaps with a short stay at Triple-A. But he never reached the major leagues. He left the organization and the game without a fond farewell.

Perhaps nine years later, the phone rang in my home. The fellow on the other end of the line identified himself. "I don't know if you remember me," he said—the standard line that I too used earlier in my life. I told him, "Of course I remember you," and proved so by providing oral outlines of some of our conversations.

He told me he now had a personal conflict, one that had to do with a relationship he was agonizing over: what to do about a woman in his life. "I thought to myself," he said, "Who do I know who'll be straight-out honest with me?" After he had provided all the particulars, I tried to be exactly that. No small talker, he thanked me and hung up the phone. I have not heard from him since.

An amazing irony unfolded as Anita and I were about to move from Manchester to Prescott. Anita loved teaching, and she was unhappily anticipating the professional void that might await her in Arizona. One of the minor league catchers in Oakland's farm system was a fellow I kept an eye on. I suspected he had been undercutting other players and back-stabbing the manager. This guy was a pet—but not mine. The pitching coach, himself subversive to some extent, I believed, had a co-conspirator. They could not sink the ship, but smooth sailing was unthinkable. Much of my time was spent trying to remedy the situation.

During that summer, the catcher heard me talking with the manager about Anita's desire to find a teaching job in or near Prescott. What his motive was, I could not be sure of at the time. In retrospect I can allow that he was just listening to his better angel. (He must have had one?)

He told me he knew a guy who was the son of the Superintendent of Schools in the small town of Mayer, Arizona. Anita and I were living in an apartment equidistant between Prescott and Mayer, while our house was being built. "I know a guy" is not an opening line I pay very much attention to. But later that day, the catcher handed me a piece of paper with the school administrator's name and telephone number. Then the closing line: "Mention my name."

Anita called; she was given—incredibly (to us)—an immediate telephone interview; she was hired to teach first grade while sitting at our kitchen table. How many wonderful gifts have reached heights that transcended, by far, the giver? I expressed my sincere gratitude to the player.

On the one hand, I did not consider him to be an exemplary person; on the other hand, his influence on our lives at the time was very significant. Still, no applause can be heard if we clap with just one hand.

I have clapped with both hands for the likes of Mike Bordick, Maddux, Moyer, Halladay, Eckersley, Ibanez, Carlos Pena, Sean Casey and others. Achievers, all. Good people, all. I am securely connected with them, yet the gland of creativity helps me choose those who have become *pets*. I cannot overlook Xavier Nady, who has fought through frustrating injuries with strength and grace. A considerate, caring young man who is a delight for me.

With complete honesty, I must say that, because of circumstance, timing, need, personality and affinity, no choice has been easier or the resultant bond stronger than the one I have with Rick Ankiel, who has suffered and who has persevered. Who has been knocked down and has risen. Whose childhood taught him the art of self-deception and self-degradation and whose later years have taught him self-awareness and self-esteem. So there he is, a favorite pet.

A few years ago, after I had finished a phone conversation with Rick, Anita said to me, "I've never seen you so emotionally involved with a player as you are with Ank." She was right. As was Oliver Wendell Holmes, whose words can conclude this chapter for me. He spoke of such relationships: "Without wearing any mask we are conscious of, we have a special face" for them.

7

Et. Al.

The Latin *et. al.*—*et. alli.*—means "and others." Those others I think of now are people—athletes—who I have had dealings with in my professional career. People who were *not* baseball players.

Many years ago, the book *Demian* by Herman Hesse was on the reading list of a literature class I taught. In the prologue, the author wrote that every man "represents the unique, the very special and always significant and remarkable point at which the world's phenomena intersect, only once in this way and never again." It is a fine thought, philosophically appealing. And yet, after years of intersecting with baseball players, *et. al.*, I have found in them the universal tendencies of 'Everyman.' The sameness. The common concerns. The similar patterns of action and reaction (often non-action) when faced with difficulties.

Happily, I accepted the opportunities offered by what I thought might be stimulating differences, not in the people but in their pursuits. The first professional female athlete I came in contact with called me at the Cleveland hotel at which our Oakland team stayed. She was in town and wanted to see me. I did not ask her who told her to call, but I did ask her who she was. Jeannie was a highly successful bowler—a top money-winner on the WPBA tour.

What did she want from me? Her inquiries were related to—men. A particular man, to start with, but it became more complicated. Jeannie was a very attractive woman but hardly self-assured when it came to inter-gender matters. She was conflicted and distracted—and bowling well below her standard.

Our telephone talks continued for years. Her game improved when she metaphorically twisted the neck off her albatross. All was well. She later married the older man who had given her my name. Was I a match-maker? Actually, I had advised against the marriage. But they seemed to live happily ever after. Not an auspicious start to my out-of-body-of-work experience. She gave up professional bowling, prematurely, I thought. I couldn't be proven wrong on that one.

Aside from one individual I maintained a relationship with for some years (she met me when I lectured her Oklahoma varsity softball team), there was only one female in my 'other' experience: an opera singer, of all things. Her husband had read something about me in the Oakland newspaper. He told her, "This is exactly who you need." Not me, literally, but what I taught.

She found me by calling the team's front office. Secretaries do not provide my number, but they did tell her what hotel I was at—and I was in Oakland at the time. She called the hotel and was connected to my room. The following day, I was to fly out of San Francisco. I told her this. "Sorry," I said. She would have none of it, asking what time my flight was scheduled for. "Noon," I said honestly. Foolishly.

"Can you meet with me at the airport at nine?" she asked. "I live right there in town." She told me she was a soprano in the San Francisco Opera Company.

I said I would meet with her, rationalizing a decision I did not want to make. "What the hell, I'll be a guinea pig in fate's laboratory." This said after I hung up the phone. (Maybe *she* was the guinea pig?)

She found me at the designated meeting place. She was, indeed, an opera diva. A *big* diva, as most opera sopranos seem to be. Our subsequent telephone relationship continued, until it came to a successful conclusion: she lost forty pounds. Oh, yes, the "one bad note" she might hit during a performance was no longer anxiety-producing, on stage or off.

An 'old guy' came to see me in Scottsdale during an Oakland spring training camp. He was my age. I put us both in our mid-fifties at the time. He was steered to me by the same fellow I'd told Jeannie not to marry. (One non-favorite guy gives me a lead for a teaching job for Anita; another gets me new clients.) This client was a golfer on the Senior Tour. He had won three times on the PGA Tour, I found out. His achievements were modest, but he was a club pro in the state of Washington—and a very happy-go-haywire guy. 'Scattered,' is the professional term I use. All over the place, as his ball too often was.

In my hotel room, he told me of his frustrations on the course. The theme was a rather complete inability to sustain concentration—to focus on task ("I hear birds chirping in the trees as I'm addressing the ball"), to respond appropriately (assessing instead of swearing), to prepare for the next shot (negative thoughts about the last shot instead of positive functional ones about the next). Essentially, he shared the weakness of many baseball players. I did know something about golf (I'll discuss that subject subsequently), so I could provide specific language that he could relate to.

Another major frustration, expressed after I had chastised him for some of the behaviors he had confessed to, was: "Chi Chi does that too, and he wins!" My answer: "You are not Chi Chi Rodriguez." (Was that before or after Dan Quail was told he wasn't John F. Kennedy? Before, I'm certain now. Could Lloyd Benson have been eavesdropping in the next room?)

Any eavesdropper would have heard language that might have caused a blood rush to the face. But I had to get this man to pay attention—in the room, before he could do so on the golf course. We spent a few hours together, after which I asked if he needed the prize money from the Phoenix tournament that would start the next day. He said he did not.

"Good," I said. "So there's no reason—no excuse—for you to give one thought to results. You'll focus on the approach and the responses we've talked about. Nothing else. Score is irrelevant."

"I'll come back tomorrow night, right?" he asked.

"Right." We shook hands.

"Wish me luck," he said.

"We're not talking about luck here. Or wishing. *Thinking* right. *Doing* right. That's what it's about." And I closed the door gently—but not before he said, "You can be unpleasant." He was smiling, however.

Next night; knock on the door. I opened it. Ken shouted out, "I shot a 68!"

"Stick the score in your ass and have a seat." That was my congratulatory offering to this excited—and excitable man. I explained my remark, should his feelings get in the way of his ability to pay attention on this night. (A distinct probability.)

"Look, if you shot a 78, I would say, 'I don't care about the score; just tell me how you behaved out there today.' And you'd be relieved, because you wouldn't really want to talk about the score. Well, the only difference with a 68 is that you want to talk about it. It isn't our subject, so it doesn't matter, in that sense. I'm happy for you. Fine. Now let's talk about how you behaved out there today." End of lecture.

He did not win the tournament, but he scored well enough to be in a better position on the board than he had in recent memory (his). We talked on the phone the next week—before another tournament. "I just want to tell you that my wife and I refer to you as "Stick-it-in-your-ass Dorfman," he said.

"Charming," I said.

We met again in Washington at a later time and spoke regularly on the phone. Ken did not win before he retired, but he earned more money than he would have thought possible, though he still, apparently, did not need it. More importantly, he felt some pride from his colleagues' remarks about his new demeanor on the course.

Joe Robbie Stadium—now known as something else I surely don't keep track of —was spitting distance from Calder Race Track. The Marlins club-house man was a kind and gentle soul—and a horse player. He would run out daily and place advance-race bets at Calder. A Latino who opened him-self up to me and frequently asked for advice, he spoke accented and care-ful English very well, and he understood common sense in any language, I would guess. A smart man.

The problem he approached me with one day was not his. "I have a friend who is in great need," Carlos said. After I nodded to have him go on, he said, "This friend is a jockey. He hasn't won a race in thirty-six days. He is suffering greatly. Could you speak to him? His English is not very good."

I said I surely could speak but, "Could he understand me?"

"Most of it," said Carlos. "But he will not speak well." I told Carlos I would do my best. We set up a morning meeting for the next day—in the 'privacy' of the cluttered equipment room. (Players would not yet be at the ballpark.)

My anticipation was high. My horse-player father would have been pleased; his boy trying to help a jockey. The diminutive fellow sat on a metal folding chair I had found at the back of the room. I sat on a bucket of batting practice balls. Carlos, not present, had been exact; the jockey was suffering. A former Eclipse Award winner, he had been reduced to a self-perceived and self-perpetuated non-entity.

He would come home from the track after his work day and refuse dinner. (That, I thought, when he haltingly provided the answers to my question, is easy for a jockey to do, since what they allow themselves to eat—because of weight concerns—hardly qualifies as 'a meal.') He gave some perfunctory attention to his wife and small children and went right to bed. (Perhaps it was 7pm.) Same reactions every day to the same results at the track: poor.

He was starting to lose mounts, meaning trainers were no longer con-fident he could ride in a way that gave their horse a chance to win. We discussed his mind-set as he rode. It was very apparent that he had lost his confidence. This manifested itself in his decision-making process. Example: he would ride with extreme caution—afraid to 'hit a hole'—an opening that would allow his horse to save ground or make a timely move to the inside or outside. His aggressive instincts had been numbed, I told him. "You and your horses are running scared."

The fear was not about injury to his body; it was about further injury to his already damaged psyche. He thought everything would go wrong and he rode in a manner that assured it would. I did not invoke 'self-fulfilling prophecy.' He understood my plain English. He also understood what I meant when I told him his behavior at home was an escape. "You want to hide from the world and your bed is the safest place," I said.

We talked about what he had to do on the track and what I insisted he do at home. "Have dinner, play with the kids, go to a movie. Pay attention to others. It will be good for you and good for them. They need you. And you need the *right* you." I told him this took courage, mental strength. I could not resist my better instincts. *"Fuerte en la cabeza,"* I said, as I tapped my forehead. It got a first smile from him. (Was he thinking, "Listen to this Gringo moron"?)

He promised he would work hard at it, and I assured him I would check on him through Carlos. "Just come again, if you need to." The jockey rose from his chair and shook my hand. I remained on the ball bucket, my eyes at a level just slightly lower than his.

Carlos had been running bets for Jim Leyland, the Marlins manager. Apparently, he told Jim about my intervention with the jockey, who would be on three mounts during that day's program. Jim told him to make three win-bets "on the horses Harvey's jockey's on." Carlos informed me shortly before game time that his friend had come in second in all three races he rode.

The next day, Jim called me into his office. "I thought you were so good you could get the guy to win a few races. What's going on?" he asked with his street-smirk.

"Tomorrow Carlos will bring the horses to me," I said, and left.

The jockey has gone on to ride at bigger tracks and in big stakes races. He has again allowed his skill to work for the horse, rather than against it. He has allowed his instinctive goodness to again express itself as a husband and father. (He rode a horse to victory in a stakes race that made the horse eligible for the 2009 Kentucky Derby. His horse came in third in the Derby.)

Saving the most affecting story for last, I tell of a young man, a student at an Ivy League college, who called and asked if he could come to visit me in North Carolina. He informed met he was a high-level skier. He said he had performance issues and needed help. That is all he said, aside from helping me establish the particulars of his impending trip: date, arrival time, etc.

I was at the gate when his flight arrived. (This was prior to the security measures resulting from 9/11.) My standard meeting-someone-at-the-airport look was in order: sweat shirt, baseball hat and dark sunglasses. The passengers came down the ramp into the gate area. No one approached me. I maintained an unnatural patience. Eventually, a young man in a wheel chair rolled up and spoke my name.

We took the elevator down to street level, and he waited curbside while I got the car from the short-term parking area. Again, I exhibited a restraint that was not typical. I said nothing about the wheel chair. The thought had immediately come to mind, "Did he have a bad spill on the slopes?" It would not have been a good question.

Karl had been six years old when he and his family were involved in an automobile accident. The father was driving, the mother was in the passenger seat, Karl and a sibling sat in the rear. Only Karl was injured badly. Paralyzed from the waist down since then, he had willed himself to an assertive independence. Yes, he was a skier—on the U.S. Olympic Paraplegic Team. What was complex about his role on the team in my mind, was quite simple in his. "My practice runs are much better than the runs during races. The instructors do a great job with us physically, but no one helps us with the mental side."

I could well understand the assumption, perhaps, made by instructors. Something like mine: 'These people are so mentally tough that they have overcome tremendous obstacles to get where they are. That exceptional mental discipline defines them.' Wrong, Karl told me. At least it was wrong on the slopes. Whether it's a batting average or a score on a golf course or a time on a ski slope—a preoccupation with results gets in the way of effective thinking and behavior. And so we worked diligently on that.

After dinner, Karl pre-empted Anita and cleared his own place. He thanked her and wheeled into the living room, where we had been speaking all afternoon. He asked, "Is this where you sit with other athletes who come to see you?" I said it was not, that I met them in my office, which was downstairs in that house. "Well," he said, "That's where we'll meet tomorrow." He soon assured Anita he could manage the shower fine and retired to his room for the night.

After breakfast the next day, he gave me directions. "Just fold up the chair and take it to the bottom of the stairs." And he sat down at the top and bumped his butt down fourteen steps, to where I waited with the chair.

A wonderful experience for me, who had thought I had it tough during my early years battling asthma. Bad is never good until we see worse. But a rose is a rose is a rose. An insistent will is an insistent will. It is not necessarily measured by degree of difficulty but on degree of determination. A guy whose mental discipline put him on the boot of a single ski, going down a slippery slope at break-ass speed, still worries about "doing well" on a clock! Maybe parallel lines meet somewhere in infinity.

We maintained phone contact for years to come. He did not win medals, but, he thought, he won "another battle." I thought he had already won the war.

No professional basketball players for me. (I did work with a high school player who became a walk-on for the Tar Heels.) I do not watch professional basketball games. The athletes are amazingly talented, but, stodgy old guy that I am, I do not appreciate the way the pro game is played.

Recently, a visiting baseball player asked me if I had ever dealt with an NBA player. I told him I had been called by one of them years ago, but I refused to meet with him.

The player in front of me decided to toy with me. "Racial bias, huh?" he suggested, with a challenging smile.

"It was a white guy, Bozo," I answered. "It's about the NBA culture, not race. Those guys don't want to listen to my shit about how to play the game."

"And I do?" he said.

"You're here."

And more followed, baseball players, all.

8

Wannabees

In an earlier volume I spoke about my 'induction' into the profession of sport psychology. I was not led screaming through the door, but I certainly had to be pushed. Dragged, is perhaps the more accurate term. Karl Kuehl did the dragging. Employing a different metaphor, the dedication page of *The Mental ABC's of Pitching* says to the reader: "To Karl—who saw the trail, built the wagon and put me in the driver's seat."

In other words, Karl was active, and I was passive in this process. At the time—1984—no college programs (as far as I know) existed for the education of aspiring sport psychologists. Now, they proliferate across the country. Just as I did not seek, so now do young (and not-so-young) aspirants seek. I exaggerate, of course, but it seems as if they all contact me for direction and advice, as if I know something about the pursuit.

What I know is that graduate programs exist. What I know is that the internet can provide leads to these programs. And what I really know is that, unless the person who wishes to enter the field understands sports and, ideally, has played at a highly competitive level, he or she is not likely to be credible to the athletes. I have been called by many such aspirants.

When Karl first had the idea for the book that became *The Mental Game of Baseball*, he tried to convince me (I didn't even want to do *that*) to write it by saying, "You know psychology, you're a writer—and you know baseball." The last requirement was spoken in a way that emphasized its place in his mind: first. When he worked at convincing me to take the job with the Oakland Athletics, he dropped the appeal about my writing and replaced it by saying, ". . . and you're a teacher and communicator."

Those are the essentials I present to callers or visitors. But there is one more matter I bring up—and it is not a small one. When Pat Quinn, who was coaching the Vancouver Canucks hockey team at the time, assured an acquaintance who was just introduced to me that I was ". . . a street bum with an education," he was saying what I say now to those who would enter the profession. Athletes will not relate to clinicians; athletes do not relate to theories and doctrines and statistical probabilities. The people whose works focuses on such matters are called "theoretical sport psychologists." Athletes want someone who, whatever he's called, works in "applied sport psychology."

Years ago, I was on a symposium held on an island resort off the coast of Georgia. The gathering was made of members of AASP, the Association of Applied Sport Psychologists. As is often the case, kindred spirits find each other. In this case the thread that ran so true was our connection with professional, rather than amateur, athletes. A specialist in golf, another baseball guy (besides me) and two who were affiliated with NHL teams. The five of us heard words spoken by people who wore tags on their shirts or blouses or jackets that included "Applied," but the five of us could not accept their doctrinaire and, we thought, fanciful presentations relating to the conversion of theory into practice.

One of the group, by no means an arrogant person, thought our small band should form a new association. "We'll call it RAASP," he said. "The *Real* Association of Applied Sport Psychology." Presumptuous, but funny. His point regarding those speakers was clear enough: Get real.

Get real and stop talking in a condescending manner. Professional athletes will chew up such a pretentious ass and spit him out. Locker rooms and clubhouses are the domains of street-tough people, and, as the Salvation Army folks learned in "Guys and Dolls," they understand best the language they know. In a back-cover comment on one of my books, former major league pitcher, Al Leiter, says, in part: "It's clear most people don't want to hear the truth about themselves, but Harv gets in your face, (and) uses a few choice words to get your attention. . ."

While I have the book in front of me, I notice what former All-Star shortstop Walt Weiss had to say. ". . . He gives it to you right on the line, whether you like it or not. . ."

These remarks are offered so I can make a contrast to the style and approach of too many who have managed to get into the field of sport psychology. Some of them are in awe of the athletes. As a result, they treat them with deference, at best, hero worship, at worst. Both treatments are unacceptable and certainly not likely to produce a professional relationship. Nevertheless, it's 'out there.' I have witnessed it.

I have also seen those who are supposed to be counseling/instructing others intimidated by their clients/students. By status or by personality?

More likely by the deficiencies of the counselor/teacher. I warn aspirants, "No one can intimidate you without your consent."

All this said, the major deficit people have is lack of a profound knowledge of the sport they are attached to. They have trouble dealing with 'sport-specific, task-specific' questions. For example, a player came up to me during my first month on the job (twenty-six years ago!) and said. "I'm having a helluva time getting the job done when the count is in my favor. You know, 2-0 counts, 3-1 counts. If the count is 0-2 or there's a hit-and-run play on, I smoke the effin' shit out of the ball. What's that about?"

I have asked some people who want to enter the field how they would respond. (One told me he'd tell the player to clean up his language!) The wisest of them have remained silent or said, "I don't know." They *have* to know. And if they do, the player will recognize the truth of the assessment immediately. And consider the assessor a valuable future resource.

The final caveat I have offered to people with great emphasis. I can think of two examples of known violators. People who came to me for counsel. There are a number of others I can name who are 'out there.' Players have told me about them and how these people approach the athlete. ("A charlatan," one player said of a guy who tells every player he comes on to that he'll make him "a champion," whatever that means.)

The violation is self-promotion. The would-be giver is more important than the would-be getter. As another player put it, "It's all about him, not us." Money, prestige—and a reputation that will advance both goals, corrupt some in the field. But they cannot fool the players. Though only a few try, none of us can. Whatever players might say (and more often, don't say) to the individual offender, they spread the word among their teammates and colleagues. That reputation prevails in the mainstream. Still, there are enough easy marks, as P.T. Barnum knew so well, to support the avaricious few who take advantage of naiveté.

"Physician heal thyself." How can a person truly help others if he cannot help himself. Reading years ago about the reasons psychologists and psychiatrists chose to pursue such careers, I was not surprised to be informed that their number one reason was past exposure. They had been on others' couches. They wanted to sit in the big chair.

There is nothing wrong with that, taken in isolation. A very great number of sound and grounded people are walking around without ever having had professional psychological intervention. And a great number could use some help. Seeing a professional does not guarantee anything. Seeing an ineffective professional does.

Where am I going with this? Players mostly want instruction and clarity and strategies to help them perform better. Many have compelling personal issues, but most (an anecdotal-statistical statement) do not. I just help them see what they're doing that doesn't work, formulate a plan of what to do next time—and implore them to discipline their minds (and harness their emotions) so they can focus on that task, in order to succeed.

Easy to say, hard to do, as the players often remind me. As if I need reminding. But the final point on this matter is that it is *not* easy to say if the sayer does not know what needs saying. Or *when* it needs saying. Or *how* it needs saying. "Touch." The word the world's great chef's use when asked about their special abilities. Anyone can own a cookbook; not everyone has the right touch. A sensitivity to others helps in its development. That means caring more about the other guy than about yourself.

I think now of some of the people in baseball who do what I did—when I was with teams—and I am proud for them. My replacement when I left the Marlins was a pitching coach with one of our minor league teams. His educational background included a degree in counseling. But that was not the major reason I recommended to the General Manager that he get the job. (I had asked the individual first, to make sure he even wanted it.)

Brian Peterson is smart, sensitive—and knowledgeable about the game, as one would suspect, since he was coaching at the professional level. He is gentler than I am, I have been told (I knew that). All that would mean to me is that his delivery is less aggressive than mine. What would not be acceptable is the definition of gentle as "non-confrontational." If something is there, go after it, and Brian apparently did, since, when Dave Dombrowski moved from Florida to Detroit to become President and General Manager, he asked Petey to come with him. He's been on the job with the two organizations for twelve years now.

A fifty-eight-year-old man called me wanting to visit. "I'd like to pick you brains," he said. He was polite, humble in tone and style—and, after all, fifty-eight. No kid with a new grad degree in sport psychology, ready to fill every jock in the universe with his package of wisdom.

Jack came to North Carolina. A gentleman, as in "gentle man." Smart, articulate, highly motivated—and he was already in the field. He had written a small, sensible book (*The Mindset for Winning*) and had worked with individual amateur athletes and a few professionals. He also had a brief tenure with a major league organization. His desire was to get back into professional baseball.

Because team officials call me (more frequently than I realized until I gave this some thought), asking if there is someone I know they can hire "who does what you do," I am in a position to provide leads for those in whom I have confidence. There are very few. Since I have never seen any of them 'in action,' my evaluation is incomplete.

A team called shortly after Jack's second visit. (He had come again, to continue our discussion about responsibilities, difficulties, dangers, approaches and the like. But, most of all, we talked about the game, the specifics of which were not his strength). The caller was a former player I had a previous connection to. (He was the guy who told a newspaper interviewer I was "brutally honest.") I told him about Jack—and warned this man, now a Director of Player Personnel—that Jack was soft-spoken. "His style (the one this guy was used to) is not like mine. So what?" I said.

I gave Jack the telephone number to call and the name of the person he would talk to. They spoke on the phone and the team official called me shortly after. "He sounds too soft," he said. I told him: "Sounding soft and being soft are two distinctly different things. Let me tell you that this guy was a Marine. Let me tell you that he had a difference with a General Manager and he told the guy straight out what he thought." To no avail.

But another team called, Jack was interviewed and given a three-year contract. He was offered an opportunity with another organization and took advantage of it.

Bob Tewksbury pitched in the major leagues for thirteen years. An All-Star who was plagued by a shoulder that caused his performance to be less than what it might otherwise have been, he compensated for the physical deficit by enhancing his mental approach. He was introduced to me by a teammate, Terry Steinbach, who was a pal of mine from our days with Oakland. Tewks and I would meet on the field before games. We each made our last 'appearance' on the field in 1998.

A short time later, he called to ask me what I thought about his possible pursuit of a graduate degree in sport psychology. He lived then, and still does, in New Hampshire and would enroll in the program offered by Boston University. I was excited, and I told him I thought he was a terrific candidate for future employment in the field. We talked frequently on the phone. After he had graduated, I received a letter from his advisor and teacher at B.U., thanking me for sending such a fine fellow and thanking me for my mentoring. (Tewks undoubtedly exaggerated.)

He has been in the employ of the Boston Red Sox ever since. Winners, all. He calls regularly, just to 'check in' or to discuss a specific situation he faces with a player. He is not soft-spoken.

I am smiling. The smile has been provoked by the story I will tell about a soft-spoken boy I met while I was with Florida. Aaron was the clubhouse boy for the Marlins Double A team in Portland, Maine. During one of my visits 1997 visits there, he approached me as I sat at my locker. He told me his goal was to be a college baseball coach. Aaron had never played the game; this I had gathered from clubhouse scuttlebutt. I took him outside to play catch the next day. Not impressive—at all.

That night, to my surprise, he played the national anthem on his violin before the game. He was *wonderful*. After the game, I approached him and told him his career path seemed clear to me. "You're an exceptional musician," I said. "I love music, I can't play any instrument and I'd cut off a nut to be able to play the way you play."

He was unimpressed. "I still want to be a coach. I've read *The Mental Game of Baseball*, and I want you to help me learn the game better." Better? I gave him no credit for knowing *anything* about the game. But this kid was the breathing example of an insistent will. He attached himself to me like a barnacle. I was not often pleased with his insistence and presence. I tried not to show it, because I admired his dedication to a dream. A fantasy? That was my take, not his.

During the fall, while I was home, Aaron called. I was initially cordial. Then I became rather silent. He told me he had "happened" to get a job as an assistant baseball coach at Brevard College. "Right in your town," he said enthusiastically. I really cannot remember my response. Eventually, I regained my composure and invited him for dinner.

He peppered his food lightly that night, but peppered me excessively— with après dinner questions. The one I recall best was about discipline. Here was an unimposing physical specimen, delicate bone structure, about 5'6" in height, a gentle demeanor, a soft voice—young. I thought, "Who the hell is going to listen to him?" Some did; some did not. He would share his experiences and I, out of compassion that was difficult to muster at times, would share my views.

One of my views was that he had better keep at his music—or I would stop talking to him. He casually took a 40-minute drive with his violin and was accepted into the Asheville Symphony Orchestra. A walk-on. He was that good.

His next stop was the University of Virginia. He became an assistant there. How did he do it? This was an ACC program, after all. I decided he must have worn out the interviewer. A call came. Aaron wanted me to come to Virginia and speak to the team. I knew he thought my visit, initiated by him, would provide some needed credibility.

"Two conditions I have. First, that you'll give a violin recital while I'm there. Figure out how to do it. Second, the Tar Heels are playing at Virginia. (I provided the date.) That's when we'll come. Get a ticket for Anita and for me—and for you, should you care to join us."

Aaron set up an evening performance that included other campus musicians: a fine pianist and a brass trio. And he played, beautifully. It was a delightful evening. The next night was almost as delightful: a jump shot from the corner to win the game for the Heels at the buzzer.

Next stop for Aaron: Emory College in Atlanta. The Harvard of the South. He was coaching pitchers. "What does he know about pitching?" I thought, ever the skeptic as I considered his qualifications. My head would fall off if he continued his improbable climb up this career ladder.

"Harvey," he said on the phone, "I'll pick you up and drive you home on the same day." A drive of approximately three and one half hours—seven, round trip.

"You know the rule," I said.

He was well prepared. He told me his parents, both professional musicians, were living in Atlanta. "You will have a private recital performed by the Weintraub trio in our music chamber (a finished basement room)."

And so it was to be. I spoke in a school auditorium to participants in all the athletic programs. It is wonderful to have a question-and-answer period with an audience of highly intelligent people. I hoped they had as good a time as I did. Aaron beamed.

I beamed that evening, when father Weintraub played two different wind instruments (not at the same time), mother played the piano and Aaron did his thing on the violin. A couple of solos were thrown in for good measure. Too bad I had to speak during the drive home.

The years that followed were filled (not exclusively, but sometimes it felt that way) with reference writing, phone interviews with school officials and phone guidance sessions with Aaron. And now he turns up in Texas. And now he's somewhere else in Texas. And now he's at a junior college. And now he's a head coach.

And then he decided to go into the field of sport psychology. Not surprisingly, he asked me to review some of the material he wrote. A number of his ideas were very original and would be effective in application, I thought. This career has seemed to be fulfilling. Aaron has visited and lectured at a few colleges with very respectable baseball programs. He has worked with individual athletes, most of them amateurs, a few professionals. I have no doubt that he has learned on the job and that he will continue to learn. And that he will broaden his professional vista and add to his professional achievements. Because he has decided it to be so.

A recent personal achievement greatly impressed Anita and me: Aaron and his wife (they married two years ago?) had twins. The pictures arrived unaccompanied by any request for parenting advice. I know this: If these babies develop the persistence of their father, they'll be able to do whatever they damn please. I hope it will please them to become musicians.

My greatest respect goes to an individual who I counseled when he was a player. A ten-year major league pitcher, Don Carman came to me near the end of his career. I will say this: his transition from a boy troubled by an extremely difficult home circumstance to a then-troubled man—to the solid, grounded person he now is, stands highest in my professional experience as an example of what a person can do for himself if he applies his concentrated energy and directed will to his daily life. The process was more demanding than most could imagine. He made the demands on himself and the results have been impressive.

After our sessions and after he left the game as a player, he, too, chose to enroll in a program that offered a graduate degree in sport psychology. A few year ago, I told Scott Boras (it was contract time and he was asking me for another three-year commitment), "I'm not getting younger, you know. It's time to think about a replacement for me." Scott does not like it when I talk about that. But I convinced him that, with the number of players being added to our client list, "someone else is needed now." I told him I thought that 'someone' should be Don Carman.

Don was, initially, called my 'assistant.' Since 2007, my travel has been curtailed. Don is a colleague, dealing with young minor league players who, by now, have become major leaguers. He flies his busy butt all over the country while I sit on mine at home. The players he deals with all appreciate him and value his connection to them. He is very effective. And now, accepting only one-year contracts from Scott, it is even clear to him that Don is the 'heir apparent.' (Don was recently given a four-year contract.)

The few people I have named have jobs many covet. They are the wanna-bees who *are*. There are so many wannabees coming out of schools with degrees and desire who never will be. I tell young men and women to try to get into college athletic programs; there are so many more of those than there are professional organizations. Their audience will be younger and more likely more open to someone so close to their own age. And amateurs will be less threatened by a professional who they know nothing about.

It is a very limited and difficult field to break into. Here I am, near the end of a long professional career, a never-wanted-to-be.

9

When My Wits Went Wandering

After having completed and proofread the previous chapter, my thoughts turned inward—to that large space in the internal galaxy where junk floats about crashing into other junk. My thoughts crashed into what I read as a misrepresentation of my true self. More accurately, my *entire* self.

An anecdotal memoir should, I believe, be filled with stories of events experienced, people met and resolutions achieved—or not. That has been my intention, at least. But aside from the first volume of this trilogy, which predominantly dealt with years spent in relative isolation, my stories, as I stand back and review them, make me uncomfortable in this sense: they seem to infer that I am a social animal, aggressively out-going and securely connected with people. Professionally, this is mostly true. Personally, it is entirely false.

So my mind wanders in an inner galaxy, seeking to sort out that 'junk'— philosophies and interpretations—the "fiery exhalations," that Aristotle believed to be the cause of the Milky Way. As a result, I have a chapter developing in my mind that is a departure from those that precede it. I hope its intent and meaning can be seen without requiring the use of the Hubble Telescope.

Off I go into a wild, blue yonder.

So as not to 'bury the lead,' let me reach for my notebook and immediately type what I wrote in it more than thirty years ago, the words written by Sir Max Beerbohm, an English parodist: "I would make myself master of some small area of physical life," he said, "a life of quiet, monotonous simplicity, exempt from outer disturbances."

Beerbohm's is a precise description of my early years as a bed-ridden asthmatic. My bedroom—the bed itself—was the area of my limited "physical life." Its limitations are obvious. What was not limited were my inner experiences. Books, radio and conversation with adults provided abundant material for thought. Circumstance provided abundant time for introspection. My infrequent attendance at school allowed the opinions and images that I shaped and painted, whether ugly or beautiful, to be formed without the influence of peer pressure.

Naturalist and writer Loren Eisleley wrote, "Outward circumstances are no substitute for inner experience." Those early years shaped that belief for me—and it endures. I remember going back to the house I lived in during my college days, when there was a time gap between my classes. I would get into bed—and contemplate my personal universe: review, evaluate, plan, decide. The solitude served me then and serves me still. And I seek it more as I get older—and, happily, it is found more easily as each year passes. The older I get, the more my life is lived inside my head.

Many years ago, as I've remarked upon before, Anita said to me, "You'd be happy living in a cave." (And Father Prior of a Carthusian Monastery, as noted in Chapter One, told me I would make a good monk.) After marriage to me for a few years, Anita began to recognize my reclusive tendencies. Some would call it 'anti-social.' She did—initially. My semantic stance argues that view. It is not what I am *against* that matters, but, rather, what I am for. Nevertheless, I look into both ends of my own small telescope, putting some things at a distance and bringing others close.

As an English teacher almost thirty years ago, I had my students examine a number of Francis Bacon's essays. One of them I just re-examined myself: "On Friendship." In the opening sentence, Bacon provides and supports the view expressed by an unidentified source: "Whosoever is delighted in solitude is either a wild beast or a god." In an earlier volume of this trilogy, I wrote about my assurances to a fellow named Jim Coburn, who wanted to know if I considered myself to be a saint or an asshole. I responded to Coburn question then as I would now to Bacon's similar either-or orientation: I am what I determine I need to be.

Bacon's extremes are less negotiable. How can a person who has devoted more than fifty years to teaching, coaching, counseling (and, in some cases, healing) people be a beast? How can a person who has numerous foibles, weaknesses, vulnerabilities and peccadilloes and (I'll allow it here, for the sake of argument) anti-social attitudes and behaviors be a god? Case closed.

I may be called whatever one chooses to call me, but hardly anyone can call me "friend." At least, according to *my* definition. A friendship, to me, is a very demanding relationship. I have great respect for it, but I never had the time for it. And I never had the urge to make the time. I have neither the desire nor the need; it's that simple.

I do have an intense concern for those people I have come in contact with because of professional circumstance. But clients are not company, faces just facilitate identification and talk is a matter of moment, and then I move on. I do not abandon, I not reject. I move on. I move back, when and if such change in direction is warranted.

Mine is the "great commitment" Dag Hammarskjold spoke of, one that "can all too easily shut our hearts" to friendship. Such an intense professional involvement can sometimes produce, he said, "a great hardness of heart." I plead guilty. The truth of the matter is that I have no heart at all for social interaction. I have answered the often-asked question of many who have not understood my RSVP regrets, whether formal or informal. I referred them to the words of the writer, Somerset Maugham: "I find social intercourse fatiguing," a view frequently expressed in these memoirs.

Back to Bacon, who was convinced that a true friend enables the other to "impart griefs, joys, fears, hopes, suspicions, counsels, and whatsoever lieth on the heart to oppress it . . ." I'm fatigued just *writing* those words. He's singing a song of love that's not for me, to paraphrase one of the Gershwin boys.

An anomaly is a "departure" from the norm. Some have so labeled me, according to the norm *they* have established. But my behavior is consistent with the norm *I* have established. At the field, I have been engaged and engaging. But when the coaching staff invited me to dinner (and I liked the coaches), I declined and retreated to my room. To regenerate, to reflect, to relax. To be by myself.

After the Marlins won the seventh game of the 1997 World Series, the clubhouse chaos was an example of uncontrolled joy and enthusiasm. Champagne poured on cigar-smoking heads, shouting, sudden friends in a frenzied embrace. I retreated to the strength coach's office with a celebratory beer in hand. I shut the door. After a time, a few players found me. They came into the room—one at a time, as it turned out—and sat down for a quiet chat. They seemed to be taking a necessary break from the other revelers.

During our years living in Vermont, a number of couples in our small town formed a social circle. All were close in age. Males in the group included two realtors, a contractor, an insurance agent, a plumber, a well-digger and, if I included myself, a teacher. But I excluded myself most often. Mike, the insurance agent, was fond of saying, "Harvey will do anything—once." He was right. I wanted to show I could enjoy their company but not that much that I would make a habit of it.

One of the realtors made what I considered to be a bizarre effort to form a bond of friendship with me. John was bright, had been in the admissions department at Fordham University before moving to Manchester. He shared common interests with me. But I did not share his very apparent need for a mutual bond.

Over a period of a month, John would sit in the library waiting for me after the school day. When he saw me pass in the hallway, he would come and escort me to the car and ask me to have a beer with him at a local hangout. Confirming Mike's 'scouting report," I did this—once. Then I told John I could not be counted on to involve myself as he wished me to be involved. I heard myself speaking like a high school kid rejecting an adolescent dating overture from an undesirable aspirant.

Pythagoras: *Cor ne edito*—"eat not the heart." I began to see John as a stalking cannibal. A very civilized one. (He would use a napkin after having gobbled an aorta.) I took myself off his menu.

The wife of a high school pal (they had married early) said I had "disappeared." Thirty five years later, I reappeared, or, to put it more accurately, they rediscovered me. (I was with the Oakland A's and had become a somewhat public entity.)

In the community in which I currently reside, some have taken to calling me "the phantom." Many activities are held in this community. The people, many retired, are caring and good people, for the most part. But I do not share their interests and concerns, as I discovered at the Wednesday night poker game Anita strongly encouraged me to attend. (Mike would have raised his eyebrows had he known: I went four times. That was more than enough.)

Walking to the end of our long driveway to pick up the newspaper and put the mail in the box, I encountered a man taking his morning walk. He slowed down to greet me. We exchanged 'good mornings' and he moved on slowly as he said, "Welcome to the community." I had been living here for eleven years.

My having been in and out of the hospital the past few years has made it a bit easier for Anita to provide excuses that would qualify as valid, excusing me from gatherings we had been invited to. Last year, at Christmas time, I showed up at a neighbor's door with Anita. The hostess met us, embraced me with a great fervor and offered an extremely enthusiastic appreciation for my attendance. Was I Nelson Mandela, arriving at her home after twenty-seven years in prison? (I would only be incarcerated for three hours that night.)

My behavior is generally (almost always) socially proper. I am civilized, after all. As I told Anita many years ago, I know how to act; I am a good actor. That's what teachers do, that's what I do when I 'inter-act' with players, clients. But I am relieved to quit the stage—glad to go through a host's door, on the way out, after a social engagement. Adoring more, in that context, the sun setting, rather than the sun rising.

I think of the story about Charlie Chaplin. This, too, I told to Anita years ago, explaining how similar, if not exact, his attitude was to mine. It was said that Chaplin could be the most charming of men to strangers sitting at the next table in a restaurant. Hello, goodbye. Rarely was that charm sincerely in evidence, except on the screen. At work. Acting.

Before I end this chapter, I am bound by a desire to be accurate. A number of people are authentic friends. Those people are the 'old friends' that share a history. We may see each other once or twice a year. A few, even less frequently. A few have passed on. "One friend in a lifetime is much," John Adams thought. He would seem to define 'friend' as I do. It is a very demanding and exacting role, and I have reservations about my effective playing of the part. I have tried when I was moved to do so. I think the significant other has trusted my sincerity, if not my constancy. And, as true friends would, they understand my limitations.

Willie Nelson sings, "There's worse things than being alone." Aloneness is where I find cosmic stillness. I found it waiting for me every day during my early years; as my health improved and I met the world beyond my bedroom, I had to sacrifice much of the stillness. I want it back now. Each day now, I find more of it. More serenity; less fatigue.

10

North of the Border

Though the term 'friend' resides uncomfortably in my limiting lexicon, my association with Carlos Tosca must be defined as a friendship. Whatever else this term means to me, loyalty is part of the definition. (Also, a friend in need is a friend to heed.)

Carlos and I spent much time together when he managed in the Florida Marlins minor league system. I saw in him the potential for extraordinary leadership. So did the farm director, John Boles. He asked me to spend a considerable amount of my time mentoring. Carlos, as I have said before, is cerebral but sensible, thoughtful but quick-witted, kind—but quick-tempered. In the past, he had not controlled his anger well; now he does. I can understand that, because it has been one of my own life-lessons.

Born in Pinar del Rio, Cuba, in 1953, Carlos and his family (he has an identical twin brother) came to Tampa when he was a boy. His father became a beloved figure in the community, a doctor who continued to work into old age and literally died on the job. A strong work ethic was important—and demanded of the sons, as one would suspect.

During his years managing in the minor leagues, Carlos prepared himself, fighting a common managerial tendency: resentment of pitchers (has Lou Piniella ever won that battle?). Pitchers who blow a game that everyone on the team has already put in their theoretical win column are not beloved. (The loss is entered for posterity on the manager's record, and resentment accompanies the taint, until the manager gets his priorities straight.)

That was one of the most daunting challenges Carlos faced—and won. In 2002, he was offered and accepted the position of manager of the Toronto Blue Jays. J.P. Ricciardi, formerly a scout with the Oakland A's, and a fellow with whom I had a fairly close relationship, had become the General Manager of the Jays. Fifty-three games into the 2002 season, he fired manager Buck Martinez. The team's record at the time was 20-33. (The previous year, Martinez's team was 80-82.)

Carlos called and told me the good news. He also asked if I could "drop in" and spend some time with him and the players. (His pitching coach, Gil Patterson, was also an old pal from Oakland days.) It was a request I could not refuse. The truth of the matter was, I looked forward to being around a team again, having dealt only with players on an individual basis since 1999. In hotel rooms or in my home office. No smell of grass there. No roar of crowds. No on-the-scene 'action.'

Gil immediately called a pitchers' meeting when I arrived at the clubhouse in Toronto. (He did so every time I showed up.) Much time was spent with Carlos in his office, at restaurant tables and behind batting cages. We were both enjoying the experience. We were enjoying each other, I can say with some certainty. Situations came up that were new and demanding. We brainstormed.

During my first series in Toronto, J.P. took me up to his box to watch the games. Also there was a man who traveled with the team as a security guard, a former cop. A statistician was also omni-present. J.P relied on him. I had an aversion to him. (J.P. eventually had a falling out with him and fired him. His name is Kevin, I think, and he is a now a 'pundit' on ESPN and who knows where else?) A third regular in the box was a member of the team's Board of Directors. An older man, he was, as were all the others, negative and critical of the players' every action during the game. He, particularly, spent much of the time pontificating on aspects of baseball about which, it was obvious, he knew little or nothing.

The atmosphere was stifling. My self-banishment was a relief to me—and to them, I'm sure. Especially after the old windbag asked me what I thought of one of his epiphanies, and I answered, "I think you're full of shit."

J.P. had asked me to make an initial presentation to the staff and they were receptive. The bullpen coach, who I have written about, was a pitcher I'd been very involved with when he was with the A's organization. Gil and, of course, Carlos, also had a shared history with me. The others were affable strangers.

The Toronto Director of Player Personnel also had an Oakland connection. Dick Scott was a Triple A player at Tacoma when I first met him. One of his favorite stories involves his coming to me for advice when he was struggling to get to the major leagues. He claims he asked me what he could do to help his career and I said, "You'd make a good coach." Whatever he felt at that moment, he soon after became a player-coach at Tacoma. Then he became a minor league manager. A good one. J.P. brought him along to Toronto, where Dick developed an excellent minor league system.

My visits, in retrospect, were more frequent than I realized at the time. My involvement included the training staff. The strength coach was a favorite. Jeff Krushell aka "Krusher" reminded me of Rick Slate, a fine young man who was the strength and conditioning coach for the Marlins when I was with that team. (Slate is currently with the Mets.) Both were young, conscientious and capable. They took their responsibilities seriously and had a genuine concern for the players' well-being.

The player I became most attached to (it is fair to say he attached himself to *me*) was Roy Halladay. He and his best pal, Chris Carpenter, approached me outside the dugout one afternoon before the scheduled stretching time for pitchers. They went beyond the territorial borders of their profession with their questions. These guys wanted to know whatever could be known. I became almost as excited as they had been.

That first 'instructional' period provided a 'key'—a trigger word for them. I had asked them both what they thought when a particular game situation arose. After each one gave his answer, I said, "Jerk!" They laughed heartily. (I then provided an appropriate answer, of course.) "Jerk" became their key. When they would have a counter-intuitive thought in the dugout or on the mound, they would say the word—and that would help to lead them to a thought that would be productive.

Halladay's wife had bought him *The Mental Game of Baseball*. He said it had opened up a world he never realized existed. When I gave him *The Mental ABC's of Pitching*, he was ecstatic. It is attached to him the way a Most-Wanted is attached to an FBI agent. His success speaks to his talent, but he often speaks of his now highly-developed mental approach to pitching.

Carpenter struggled with a damaged shoulder and other injuries, but when he is healthy and able, he is an extremely effective pitcher. He signed with St. Louis as a free agent. (He won the Cy Young Award in 2005.) Roy signed a long-term contract with the Jays. (He had won the award in 2003.) This year, as a free agent, he signed with the Phillies.

In the very competitive Eastern Division of the American League, the Blue Jays, with its limited budget, could not realistically compete with the Yankees and Red Sox. They became a perennial third-place team. Before Carlos Tosca and after him. But in Carlos's only full season as manager in Toronto, 2003, the team won 86 games (losing 76). Very respectable. Carlos was doing an excellent job, in my view. He communicated with players' and confronted difficulties immediately and effectively; he balanced discipline and order with respect for players' individuality and self-sufficiency. He was a leader.

Is this bias? The first principle of existentialism is that man is nothing else but what he makes of himself. Carlos had been exemplary in that regard. He had made himself a very good major league manager, and I fail to see that evaluation as biased. The following season, after 111 games, J.P. failed to see what I—and many impartial observers—saw. He fired Carlos.

When he was initially hired, many of the baseball 'experts,' television talk-ing-heads and newspaper nuisances decried the fact that Tosca "had never played the game in the major leagues." (He hadn't played in the minors ei-ther, but that did not seem to trouble anyone.) Walt Alston was able to have a very successful 23-year managerial career with the Dodgers. Attributable to the fact that he played in the major leagues—and had *one at-bat* with the Cardinals? (He struck out.) This often-expressed caveat for managerial can-didates is typical of critics (deaf piano tuners, Saul Bellow called them).

A great value such sport-section writings have is as liners of a cat's litter box the next day. It is easier to find a pink diamond than it is to find a baseball man's opinion that is supported by logic—or common sense. (OK, that's a bit hyperbolic.)

Yet sometimes nay-saying pundits, to their credit, do come around to see what is in front of their faces, rather than what's in their big box of gener-alizations. Carlos began to get credit for doing a good job.

Why, then, was he fired? Why is any manager fired? For good reasons, for bad reasons, for no apparent or revealed reasons at all. But I'll just give my take on this case, an opinion which, I acknowledge, cannot be supported by logic or common sense. The only person who can have a real sense of it is the man who made the decision. And he has that sense, only on the condi-tion he is being honest with himself. To expect high level corporate officers to be honest with the media or the public is to expect to be disappointed. I cannot know how honest they can be with themselves, since people always tend to feel better when they can justify their behavior.

Let me offer just one explanation I read regarding the termination of Carlos's tenure with the Blue Jays: A communication problem existed. Say what?

I'll say what I believe: J.P. hired Carlos without realizing how strong a personality he was. Did he think Carlos would be so grateful for the job that, beholding to his boss, he would be a yes-man? That he would be ac-cepting of every decision made or point of view expressed by his General Manager? Only the General Manager knows the answer, but I have my opinions, don't I?

I think J.P. was unpleasantly surprised. I was witness to an exchange at a Toronto restaurant after a game. The three of us went out for a few drinks and Carlos had a few too many. His tongue became loose and it wagged quicker than his brain modified and toned down its message. (A fairly ac-curate one.)

The discussion gained heat as a result. The topic addressed the team's need for players who could do the job better than a few on the roster. The General Manager manages the purse and Toronto did not have a full one. The prevailing impression after the night had ended was not left by the content of the debate but by the heightened intensity of one of the debaters.

I remember thinking that this night did not serve Carlos well. Correction: Carlos did not serve himself well.

In deference to fairness, I must say that I was not present often enough to consider my judgment of his firing as complete or final. But just as a police composite drawing of a criminal's description can capture the essential look of the criminal (and, often, the man himself—or women herself), so have I drawn my composite, based on what I observed and heard. Carlos was not a push-over. Perhaps he was difficult at times. Perhaps he was a nuisance—but only to J.P. Life would be easier without him than with him. The team's record was 47-64. The trigger was pulled.

Someone always takes the hit. Players are usually protected from the assaults of administrative action. Players make too much money. One cannot swallow their contracts easily and there is no Heimlich Hug strong enough to dislodge so many dollar bills. And General Managers do not fire themselves. So that leaves. . . . Right.

All this having been said, what burns my ass, aside from a three-foot high fire, is the duplicity of people who provide the media and fan base with bogus, contrived explanations. A problem with communication? Not with the players, as implied. It is Carlos's strong suit. (He is, by the way, bi-lingual, a great asset, since Toronto, like all teams, had a number of Latin players.) Between manager and General Manager? If so, say so.

Players tend to cover their own rear ends also. (I think only red-bottom monkeys can't be accused of doing that.) Because Carlos was replaced by one of the coaches (who has since been fired), the players were careful not to put themselves in the new manager's doghouse. But those who contacted me supported their departed manager without my solicitation. The strength coach was particularly perplexed by the managerial change. (He left the Jays to set up his own athletic academy in British Columbia.) Joe Torre had nothing but good things to say about Carlos. (He had chosen him for one his All-Star coaching staffs.)

What am I thinking at this very moment? I am thinking of Madeline Kahn, playing a dance hall bimbo in the film, "Blazing Saddles." I am hearing her sing, "I'm tired. . ." That's how I feel right now. A baseball bimbo, tired of writing about this annoying memory. But I need to take it to its conclusion.

I was supposed to meet the team in Cleveland when I learned of Carlos's firing. I called the traveling secretary to tell him to cancel my room at the hotel. I was not coming to Cleveland. I did not call J.P. Ricciardi. It would not be appropriate (or smart) to communicate when consumed by anger. J.P did not call me. Dick Scott did call. I made my unhappiness clear to him, in a surprisingly calm tone of voice. He spoke of my past relationship with Carlos. Implicit in the remark was the suggestion of bias. "Oh, so I'm pissed because of my history with Carlos?" I said. "No, I'm pissed because of the way it was handled." I reminded Dick I also had a fine relationship with J.P.—and with him—from Oakland days. End of talk.

J.P had been good to me; I had been good to *him*. But that was not relevant to the Tosca situation—at least, as far as I was concerned. Was it relevant in the view of the General Manager? Apparently so. Another caller told me he heard that J.P. had said, "I lost a lot of respect for Harvey." Because I didn't show up in Cleveland? He had expected me to? Because he saw where my loyalty had come down? It came down on the side of honesty, and I believed he was on the other side. It was not the firing of Carlos that provoked me, but the reasons espoused to the media for it.

I can't remember who said it: "One must find a way to love the world, without trusting it."

The following season, Carlos became the bench coach at Arizona, where he remained until his good pal, Fredi Gonzalez, was named manager of the Florida Marlins in 2007. Fredi asked Carlos to join him on the bench. In 2005, Carlos wrote the Foreword for my book, *Coaching the Mental Game.* We speak to and e-mail each other regularly. I have not spoken with J.P. since before 'the happening.' He knew I would stay south of the border thereafter, so he shut the door—against the wind.

But not, ultimately, against his own fate. On October 3, 2009, after eight years as Toronto's General Manager, J.P. was fired. He had hired two managers after Carlos. The results were profound mediocrity in one case and included a player rebellion in the other. J.P. was criticized for a number of free agent signings that went amuck—and for what might be described as an 'antic disposition' prior to the 2009 trade deadline, when Roy Halladay's possible fate was J.P.'s regular topic with the media.

The only consequence of the machinations was a distracted and frustrated star pitcher.

11

The Dreaded Thing

Since I have just completed writing a very unpleasant chapter, the residue of the unsettling feelings that accompanied it still darkens my mind. If one cloud is enough to eclipse the sun, what will two do my inner universe? I'll find out. Because I might as well endure a most unpleasant topic now, while the shadow lingers—and get it over with, so some light can shine again on my brain's dark waters. And so I paddle forward.

We cannot really understand something until we know what it is *not*. A player who has suddenly lost his ability to throw a ball where he wants to throw it, who continually throws it into the ground a few feet in front of him, or who launches it into space beyond the intended target is *not* having a mechanical problem. To begin with, that is. The actual issue is a psychological one, which affects the muscles and, thereby, the natural kinetic function. The cerebellum, the basal ganglia and other circuits 'short out,' so to speak.

The ability to control the mechanical movement of the arm is lost. Feeling in the nerve endings of the fingers are affected, lost most often. The ball feels slippery, if it is felt at all. The fingers grip the ball tightly, squeezing. "Like holding a grenade," many of them say. Rather than holding an egg. The legs have a strange (weak) sensation during performance. The arm tightens, slows down through the delivery. Breathing is affected. Saliva is non-existent. The muscles hear the deafening noise of a warning signal, a clanging in the brain like a firehouse bell. And the eyes focus on. . . . nothing or the wrong thing. (I have many pictures in the file of players looking up in the air, to see where they release the ball. They should be looking at the target: the receiver's mitt.)

The physical disability is the symptom; the mental disability is the problem. And it is just that: a 'problem,' a word I try to avoid in my work, but in the case of "The Thing," it is unavoidable. A *big* problem, at that. The suffering a player goes through is unimaginable to those who have not experienced the embarrassment and humiliation of not being able to perform a task executed easily by children.

One player said this to me a few years ago: "It's like being at the White House, eating dinner with all those big shots, and you can't get the spoon into your mouth. It keeps going in your eye. And everyone is looking at you thinking, 'This guy's fucked up.' And they're right."

The first experience I had with a player who suffered from what became known as "The Blass Disease" (or "Syndrome" or "The Yips") was a minor league catcher who could not throw the ball back to the pitcher. The poor kid had no prospect of becoming a major league player, even if he had not been afflicted. Originally, I was questioned by one of my superiors for spending so much time with him, but I thought that the time would also serve me—in the long run—(more than it would serve him). It was a correct presumption, and the trial-and-error intervention allowed me to become more sophisticated in the future, as I dealt with those who were 'diseased.' A few infielders were also among the afflicted.

The first major league pitcher I had such dealings with was a fellow who came from another team. He had difficulties controlling the ball, even in bullpen sessions. The problem, as always, had appeared 'suddenly.' It was precipitated by a state of mind based on the fact that he had previously been traded by his team for a star player on another team. A typical response of a pitcher (or a position player) is to feel the need to justify the trade. Many go through this.

Oakland's new pitcher had two fine seasons and one mediocre one in the three years before the trade for the star. After the trade, the burden proved too great. The two of us spent much time with each other—at the field and away from it, dining together many evenings during spring training. Talking always. He began to improve.

He reached a point, early in the season, at which the pitching coach felt he could be used in the games. We had discussed the nature of the use and I was adamant in my belief that he should be put into "non-pressure situations" exclusively. This was done; the pitcher became a middle reliever, working in games in which we were comfortably ahead or considerably behind,

His performances went well, his original difficulties considered. He became the winning pitcher in a few games in which he held the opposition for a couple of innings and we came back and took the lead, whereupon he took to the showers. Though he had thirteen wild pitches over the course of the season, his record was very respectable for *any* pitcher: 9-1 with a 3.02 earned run average.

Did we catch lightning in a bottle? Well, a small bottle, perhaps. The manager and pitching coach began to trust him—too much, I thought. My support for the pitcher was evident, but I qualified my enthusiasm. The non-pressure situations were perfect for him and served the needs of the team to have a pitcher who was 'an innings-eater.' But one day, the line was crossed; he was put into a game in the ninth inning. We had a one-run lead. He was to close the game, against my earlier warnings.

The game was lost, but the setback to the player was more important—to me. He slowly regained his confidence. The major league staff did not share it. One screw-up was enough for them. The A's did not offer him a contract for the next year. He signed with another team and pitched four more years in the big leagues, for three teams—with mediocre results. But he pitched (except for a couple of glitches) without wildness. His command was not wonderful, but, then again, neither is the command of many mediocre pitchers.

I had tried to have the young man draw a better picture of himself than the one he drew when his problem was in full bloom, before he had come to the A's camp. I tried to help him resemble the new picture. I tried to elicit behaviors that, if habituated, could grow over any of his past, dysfunctional ones. As a result of his determination and perseverance, he conquered his 'monster.' (One of my lines to guys with this problem is "Don't feed the monster, starve him.") As a result of his relentlessness, my reputation was enhanced. Life is not always fair.

Every case has some individual uniqueness. Some can be considered more dramatic that others, but to *me*, they are all dramatic, as they are to the sufferer. Nevertheless, diagnosis will dictate prognosis. The 'cure' for the disease is not easily—or often—achieved. If it is achieved at all. (I liken it to athlete's feet: keep your feet dry and the fungus will be dormant, but it's still there.) There are charlatans out there who claim they have 'the cure' in their possession. The technique that will give the player the fix he needs. I do not trust them, nor have I seen or heard evidence that convinces me otherwise. (More on that later.)

I tell people that the reason I have a reputation of being 'the guy'—as someone identified me—when it comes to dealing with this issue, is that my failure rate is not as bad as others.' Success, for me, is getting the player to compete at the level he was at before, as some of them put it, 'the shit hit the fan.'

A minor league pitching coach with the Angels asked me to come early to the Instructional League game our kids were to play against them. He had a pitcher with the curse and wanted me to take a look and offer suggestions. The coach had the pitcher throwing from his knees. He had other techniques he told me about. It is unwise to say that someone is doing something misguided when he is flying blind to begin with. We do not find ordinary solutions for extraordinary problems. We do not employ sensible techniques for problems that make no sense to us. So, as stated before, first cause must be determined before any headway can be made. And this is what I told both coach and pitcher. I don't know if any good came of it.

The good that has come from my dealings with troubled pitchers is that, while most do not get back to the level of competitive skill they had prior to their difficulties, all have been able to come away with something they value greatly: their dignity. They have been able to throw strikes—on the sidelines, in bullpens—and during games. But, as I said, their 'stuff' has not been the same. Something is missing. I believe that something to be the all-out aggressive approach that puts life on the ball they deliver. The subtle residue of uncertainty, of caution, is still there. Even those who did compete effectively were not at the level of their previous self. (Some wanted to believe otherwise, but I believe what I saw.)

A most famous example of a pitcher who suffered through the process is Sam Militello, a pitcher I dealt with while I was with the Marlins. Signed by the New York Yankees in the 1990 draft, he won the International League Most Valuable Pitcher Award in 1992, putting together a record of 12-2 with a 2.35 earned run average. After he had been promoted to the major league team and had a particularly effective performance, the famous/infamous back page of the *New York Daily News* had a full-page headshot of him with the slug, "Sam I Am."

Sam developed shoulder problems which had much to do with his subsequent difficulties. When he returned from his injury he had trouble with his command. His responses to his difficulties exacerbated the problem, to over-simplify. He was released by the Yankees after the 1993 season. The Marlins gave him a minor league contract in 1994, my first year with the team. By the time I first met him, he could rarely throw a ball close to the catcher. At one of our many lunch sessions, he brought in the *Daily News* back page, printed the day after the Yankees released him. The same headshot, but with a different slug: "Sam I Was." Clever—and hurtful.

We spent an inordinate amount of time together. For his bullpen sessions, I had a dummy hitter brought out—not a player who was foolish enough to volunteer himself as guinea pig, but am inanimate wooden dummy. Sam plunked him on a regular basis. Rick Williams, our fine and sensitive pitching coach for the Triple A team, worked caringly and conscientiously with Sam—when I was there and, with more 'hands-on,' when I was not. After months of work, a live 'batter' did offer himself to stand in.

Sam eventually pitched in simulated games, then in extended spring camp games. We spent the entire year working together closely. Very closely and very often. He pitched in Instructional League games that fall. I myself could have thrown strikes on a regular basis—but the batters would delight in my offerings. To a lesser extent, the same was true with Sam's. The life on his fastball wasn't there; his sliders and curveballs did not have a sharpness to them. He could throw strikes again. A well-deserved self-respect was evident in him.

In *Paradise Lost*, John Milton offered the thought that "nothing profits more than self-esteem. . ." Paradise wasn't found by Sam, but profit was. He also became a minor league pitching coach. He surely would be patient with his charges.

A young pitcher, a former high draft choice of the Minnesota Twins had flown out to see me while I was still working for Oakland and living in Arizona. He told me on the phone, "I can't hit a barn door." He flew to Phoenix, rented a car at the airport and made the two-hour drive up I-17 to Prescott. He would stay for a couple of days.

Anita and I lived in a house on a cul de sac at the top of a hill. No other house was near. After going down our steep driveway, I would turn left to head to town. On the right was a very high embankment, at the top of which was an unsold lot. The bank of earth was only slightly sloped, acting as a wall—but never acting. Until Steve came out. (In fact, it still never 'acted'—except as a perception in his mind.)

When Steve arrived, I greeted him at the door, took his travel bag, put it on the floor near the entrance and said, "First thing we do is play catch." His face blanched. I went into my office, grabbed two gloves and a baseball and led him back out the doorway. We walked down the driveway, and when we reached the street I waited for him to place himself.

Predictably, he walked toward the bottom of the hill. He saw the earthen wall and knew this was a perfect alternative 'catcher' for his misguided throws. If he launched the ball, it would hit the wall with a soft thud and roll to the bottom, where I could easily pick it up and return it to him. If he was the one standing with his back to the bank, I would have to run down the hill to retrieve each errant throw. An impossible situation, so, of course, the other arrangement was practical and obvious.

Obvious, but not allowable. I told him he was to stand on the upside and I would stand on the downside. The color left his face again. His thought, as he admitted later, was something similar to what I expressed to him after our catch. "You said to yourself, 'If my throw goes astray, this old guy has to go after it as it rolls down the street and then he's gotta walk back up.' You had a picture of me running down and huffing up the hill after every throw."

But this did not happen. I held up the glove, giving him a target. And said, "Right here, Steve." And it went there time after time. I would say, eight times. (I didn't want to push the test beyond its limit.) I said after the last throw, "That'll do," and walked toward him. He hadn't moved. As I waited for him at the foot of the driveway, he said, "What the hell was *that* all about?"

I told him it was about his focus being so strong on what *I* would have to do that he never gave a thought to himself. (A 2009 magazine article quotes me ((accurately, I'm afraid)): "Self-consciousness can fuck you up.") He was amazed.

For Steve, the problem began with a traumatic moment during his first major league spring training camp. Three pitchers were lined up close to each other facing three other pitchers. They were playing catch, loosening up their arms. Steve was in between two veteran pitchers, Frank Viola and Bert Blyleven. One of Steve's throw was slightly off the mark. One of the veterans (probably Viola) chastised him—in the typical mock-serious tone of big league banter. The rookie could not discern any playfulness in the rebuke. He was, as expressed in the players' vernacular, 'toast' thereafter. His throws went out of control; his mind had preceded them, of course.

Steve was released by the Twins, signed by two other teams but never made it to the major leagues. He had been a 2nd round draft choice. After his Prescott visit, he could hit a wall—and a catcher's mitt. But, too often, his pitches also hit the opponents' bats.

A former major league catcher called me from Florida. He was playing in a "40 & Older League" for former big leaguers. He could not throw the ball back to the pitcher. "Always?" I asked on the phone during our three-hour conversation. "Not always," he answered.

"When are you ok?" I asked. After some thought, he said, "When the pitcher is in trouble."

"In other words, if the pitcher is struggling, you're thinking about him. How to help him and so on. But if he's doing well, you're thinking about yourself—your throw back to him. Right?"

He said he never realized that his thoughts were so fixed on himself and the mental image of a bad throw—and the annoyance to the pitcher (plus the possible ridicule of onlookers)—that the act could not be performed naturally.

Another retired catcher was interviewing me for his post-game radio show. The interview was focused on *The Mental Game of Baseball*, but after it was completed he brought up the fact that he had trouble throwing the ball back to the pitcher during his playing days. He wondered whether I could explain it. I asked him if he knew when it had started. He said he did not.

"Do you want to know?" I said. After fifteen minutes we had identified the traumatic moment. He said it should have been obvious to him. I told him we bury what we do not want to be 'obvious.' If we choose to dig for it, we usually find it. He remembered many other moments—off the field—that were related to the on-field 'first cause.'

Some pitchers cannot field their positions well because they have a problem making throws to first base (and second, and third). One pitcher I dealt with could not throw from a stretch position in an attempt to keep the runner on first base close to the base. "Always?" I asked.

"Only when the sign comes from the bench," he said. If the pitcher decided to throw over, all went well. If the manager wanted the throw to be made, and the catcher flashed the sign, the ball and all hell broke loose.

Another pitcher tripped on the mound and balked as a result. He had three more that night and the umpire could have called three more than he did. I received a call the next day from the player. He said he had "the yips."

All manner of unique specifics could be provided, but they all have similar precursors. The first time I had any exposure to a phenomenon of this type was as a fifteen-year-old. (I wrote about the incident in a book for coaches.) I was a soda-jerk at a luncheonette in the Bronx. The owner had a sister who put in some time working there. One day he said to me, "Harvey, cross Lil; she's going home now."

He wanted me to hold her hand—as one would a child—while she crossed a major thoroughfare, Gun Hill Road. As I have written, Lil being an attractive woman and me being at an age when hormonal impulses were rampant, I was happy to comply with the request. After we reached the other side of the street, I asked her if she needed help the rest of the way, since she had three or four other streets to cross. She told me she had no trouble crossing narrow side streets such as Putnam Place or King's College Street or Tryon Avenue.

Perplexed, I said to her, "What's this all about?" She told me that when she was twelve years old, she had crossed a major road and was kicked in the head by a horse on the street. I did the math in my head. "She's 34, this is 1950. She was born in 1916; she was 12, so that was . . ."

I said to her, "Lil, that was in 1928. There are no horses on the streets anymore."

"Yes there are," she said, tapping her head.

The effort it takes for someone to prevail against traumatic memory of any kind is immeasurable. Two pitchers who stand out in my mind because they fought and won—and pitched effectively again at the major league level—are John Burke and Rick Ankiel (a previously proclaimed 'pet' to whom I will devote an entire chapter). Both fought fiercely and relentlessly—won battles and were winning the war. But this kind of war never ends; it must be fought every day. Both pitchers quit pitching. John told me, "I get up very day and have to face the demons. I know I can beat them—have beaten them—but the fight is exhausting. Playing just isn't fun."

Rick's message was essentially the same. "The energy it takes; the anticipation of going to the field with the strength you need isn't the same as going there with joy. It just got to a point where it was wearing me down mentally."

The payoff could not be appreciated because of the ordeal that was required to have it. Simply, the price was too high. Self-trust, as Emerson wrote "Is the essence of heroism." But constant heroism is neither possible, it seems to me, nor desirable, even if enacted. It can eventually erode the spirit. Failure just does it much more rapidly.

In *every* case I have dealt with, the athlete who suffered so greatly from the inability to direct a ball to a designated target—and who then was able to regain that ability—first was able to identify causality. With help, in most instances, but, assuredly, the cause became clear to each individual. And this was the case for every athlete, without exception. Some regained competitive form; most, as I have already suggested, did not.

The 2009 season provide the greatest 'success story' an afflicted pitcher has had. The particular relief pitcher flew in to visit with me. The player himself was extremely self-conscious about his inability to play catch from forty feet, to say nothing of executing pitches. His major league manager and trainer, both of whom I had past dealings, supported and encouraged the visit.

The trainer's involvement was, I believe, pivotal. The pitcher had had three elbow surgeries and extended rehab periods. Almost everyone who observed his difficulties were quick to attribute them to the physiological. *Almost* everyone. The pitcher and those around him every day knew better. But the fact that the player had a sort of 'free pass' helped, I am certain. It allowed him to rationalize the problem to an extent. And to camouflage it.

In any case, he went back to the big league club after weeks spent re-orienting himself (rehabbing, they still called it) at the team's extended spring training program. He was functional—and more. He was (and remains) extremely effective.

"Ode to Joy" still resounds in my ears. And I would like to hope that no more cases of the dreaded thing will require the music to change. I am too old for this ordeal.

Finally, a few words about Steve Blass, now a commentator for the games of the Pittsburgh Pirates, the team he pitched for. For years I heard him say he had no idea why his meltdown occurred. (Someone conjectured that it was because his teammate, Roberto Clemente died in a plane crash and Blass suffered from survivor guilt. Blass wasn't even on the plane!)

The trouble began in 1973, the year after he finished second in the voting for World Series MVP, behind Clemente. A number of years ago, a self-promoting fellow claimed in interviews that he had 'cured' Steve Blass. Of course, Blass never had the opportunity to throw another ball in competition, so that claim was all inference, no empirical evidence.

Can one say with certainty that Blass' command would come back in a game setting? Can one say with certainty that, if it could, the efficacy of his pitches would reappear? I can say with certainty that the claim was never tested. It could be possible—in the hypothetical sense—but dozens of clients over a couple of dozen years have led me to believe otherwise. Of course, the possibility exists that I might not have the skill to do what this fellow *guarantees*. (A teammate of his once asked Walt Weiss for concrete assurance regarding something he wanted Walt to do. Walt said to him, "If you want a guarantee, buy a toaster.")

Cavalier certainty aside, what remained objectionable to me was a further claim, in the form of inference: 'If I can cure the guy this disease is named after, I can cure anyone' (and quickly, by the way). Enough said about the claimant. There is more to be said about the problem, but this is not a technical manual. And it is not useful or pleasant to expand on the topic. I will conclude by stating what Madison Avenue advertising agencies know so well: an innocent consumer is an easy mark. Especially if he is desperate.

And "The Thing" brings dread, despair and desperation to all those it stalks.

12

Illusions of Grandeur

I taught Ibsen's play, "The Wild Duck," to my high school Advanced Placement English students. They understood well the playwright's theme: Take away a man's illusion and you rob him of happiness. In my most recent years I have committed occasional robbery. It was neither the intent of the robber or the robbed. Irrespective of intentions, this kind of holdup will never happen again.

The first connection with a high school student since my teaching days came about because I allowed myself to be trapped. The 'student' was a baseball player; that's why I was called. The telephone rang in my room at the Marriott Marina in Ft. Lauderdale. I was with the Florida Marlins at the time. The call went something like this:

"Hello, Mr. Dorfman. My name is Mr. So-and-So. I'm calling from Orlando. I'm hoping you could work with my son, who's a very talented high school pitcher."

"I'm very sorry, Mr. So-and-So, I don't deal with high school players. I'm too busy and, besides, I don't live in Florida, so geography is another issue. I live in North Carolina."

"Where in North Carolina, Mr. Dorfman?"

"A bit southwest of Asheville."

(Excitedly) "*We* live in Asheville!"

(Inaudible groan.)

"Mr. Dorfman, did you hear what I said? We live in Asheville; we're at a baseball camp in Orlando."

"Yes, I heard."

"Well, maybe after the season we could come by. What might your fee be?"

(Caving in, but presuming this would be a one-visit-experience.) "Give me your number; I'll call if I have the time. There won't be a fee should you come."

(Fast forward to October.) Anita hands me the home phone, whispering, "It's a Mr. So-and-So. He says you wanted to talk with him."

(Inaudible groan.) "Hello, Mr. So-and-So."

The rest, as is often said, is history. The mother and father both came with their purportedly precocious young son, who, I must say was a wonderful kid: smart, attractive, polite and understated. As opposed to his father, who was, I saw, embarrassing the 15-year-old boy with a hyperbolic testimonial regarding the boy's athletic prowess. The mother had brought a cake and sat quietly, an observer, though, I suspected, not an entirely innocent one.

The question of fee arose again. (The family had some means, it was clear.) I said there would be no fee. This after all, was a one-time meeting, right? Wrong. The boy was so compellingly innocent and humble and smart and ---- I buckled. We set up another meeting.

The following spring, Anita and I attended one of his summer league games in Asheville while I was home on a break. He held his own against older competition, coming in to pitch an inning in relief. Though he struck out two of the three batters he faced, his stuff was hardly 'electric'—something that would catch a scout's eye.

The father called often. Too often. I became curt and impatient, but he had a single-mindedness which pre-empted any sensitivity he might have to my reactions. He just wanted to talk about his boy.

Both parents appeared at the house when the boy came for another visit. And another. No cake the second time. Flowers. The next time, their pick-up truck arrived loaded with mulch, which the father spread very nicely in the flower beds, thank you, while the boy and I were engaged in our meeting. Anita and I were embarrassed, actually. The father should have been.

He relentlessly took his son to major league show-case gatherings, to camps, to any place the boy could possibly learn something or be on display. Somehow, our relationship continued, irregularly after a time, for four years. During those years, the father transferred his son to a different high school because of an antagonism with the coaching staff. The father's explanation was, of course, a condemnation of others and a defense of his own point of view. I had no involvement, so I could only listen—and hold an unexpressed opinion, based on what I knew about one of the antagonists.

During the lad's senior year, after I had seen him play in a high school league game, I called one of my pals, a colleague working for the Scott Boras Corporation. He is a 'contact man'—meaning he scouts young players, talks to their families and encourages those players he evaluates as worthy to enter into a relationship with Boras Corp.

At the time Bob Brower lived in Durham, North Carolina. I asked him to drive west to watch 'my kid.' The boy was held in very high regard in his school. He was an outstanding student, a fine citizen, good looking, personable and popular. He would be a perfect poster boy for his high school. Prom king and so on. But I did not see the compelling precocity required in a player whose goals were set as high as his: set, in all probability, by his father. "Bob," I said to my friend on the phone. "Just give me your take on this kid. And be honest; I have no vested interest here."

The truth, according to my compliant observer-friend, was that the boy did not project enough talent for us to have an interest. Boras Corp. players are high-end athletes, so to say he did not interest our evaluator does not mean he did not have *any* talent.

As Lord Byron put it: "Time! The Corrector where our judgment err. / The test of Truth. . . ." And nothing can be meaner than the truth. The father's and the son's judgments about the boy's prospects did not hold up to that test. One of their aspirations had been to be offered a baseball scholarship by a major college, one with a formidable program. That goal was never reached. Instead, the boy enrolled is a small school.

The frequency of my telephone contact diminished. With the boy, that is. The frequency of the father's calls increased to a disconcerting extent. What did he want? Reassurance? Sympathy? The advice I tried to offer went in a direction that was west to the father's east, insofar as the itinerary he had mapped out for his boy. I blessed the player who had sent me a caller-ID telephone attachment as a Christmas gift. When my conscience allowed, I ignored the father's excessive attempts to contact me.

Eventually, everything 'went south' for the family. I learned from a call the young man made to me the following year that his parents had divorced and that he was no longer on speaking terms with the father. The mother, it seems, had just been along for the ride but had recognized the wrong course and asserted herself. It didn't work.

The father's calls continued. He was in denial and I told him so. I stopped answering all his calls in the future. Eventually, the attempts stopped. The boy contacted me a couple of years later. He was doing well—at a college he had transferred to. He told me he was no longer playing baseball, but thought he might try to play again the following spring. For the fun of it, if fun could be found. Maybe he would transfer schools again. He asked for some ideas about alternate small colleges. A few possibilities were discussed. I have not heard from him since.

This is the signature story about overzealous parents—fathers, mostly—of precocious sons. Rather, sons they *believe* to be precocious. The judgments are often (most often?) based on what the proud papa *wants* to see, rather than what can actually be seen. That illusion ultimately leads to a stark and painful reality. The cliché 'rude awakening' applies.

Other experiences have been uniquely similar, if that makes oxymo-
ronic sense. Same body, different face. Same parental type, different style.
But—same illusion and *same* result. Without exception, every high school
kid whose parent sought me out fell short of the parent's judgment of the
son's talent and of his potential to reach the level of elite competition they
both sought.

I have an on-going relationship with a boy who fits the mold, with one
very important distinction: mother was always skeptical and father came
down to earth quickly. He had his sights set on a scholarship to Clemson
for his boy. After watching the son play, I told them it wouldn't happen. No
qualifying language. This was as clear as could be—to me. The boy ended
up at a small school in Tennessee, playing sparingly. My willingness to get
involved with him was based on a learning disability he had. I was more
interested in helping him cope with that. So was the mother. Tensions in
the marriage put the relationship on precarious grounds, but the father, as
I noted, adjusted his views and behaviors. With special assistance provided
by the school, Jon is fighting his way through his college experience. Successfully, as it stands right now.

Six years ago, I picked up the phone to hear a woman's voice. She had
taken her son to an athletic facility in Asheville, where a former big leaguer
advised her to call me, saying that I lived close-by. I had quite enough to
keep me busy and my past experiences with parents and high-schoolers did
not motivate me to have any more of them. This one had an intriguing difference however. The boy was a basketball player.

I did not find this out immediately. The mother began with a rapid-fire
explanation of circumstance that precipitated the call. She told me where
she had taken here son and who had said, "You've gotta call this guy." The
guy, now on the other end of her phone line, said he was too busy.

Another spontaneous and foolish remark: "And besides, my fee is too
steep."

She responded, again rapid-fire: "I'll pawn my wedding ring."

For chrissake, here we go again. Another crazy, I thought.

Not so crazy, but extremely aggressive. She finally got around to the point
that her son was an outstanding basketball player, a senior in high school
whose goal was to win a scholarship and play in a major basketball program. The idea of working with a basketball player appealed to me because
---- he was *not* a baseball player and, having coached the sport, I was titillated by the prospect of doing so again, on an individual basis.

The mother had introduced herself by name and later mentioned that an
older son was playing at Kansas. The name registered, and I was encouraged. A good bloodline, though the older son was not a 'star.' A residue
of reluctance remained, despite the mother's enthusiastic assurances that

her son was "a good boy and an eager learner." I fired my final shot over her head, trying to scare her away. It missed badly. She accepted my stated fee without hesitation. (She did not have to hock her ring; she drove a Porsche.)

The boy came to the house. He was painfully shy, volunteered little and answered my questions with skeletal responses: no meat on the bones. He was polite and attentive, so I allowed that to define his 'goodness.' Innocent until proven guilty.

After a number of get-togethers, I went to see him play. It had been some time since Anita and I attended a high school basketball game, and we both enjoyed the atmosphere once again. We arrived early—halftime of the junior varsity game—and sat in the area the mother had designated on the phone. They found us easily and greeted us warmly. She sat on one side of me, Anita on the other. The dad sat next to his wife. He was a big man, in height and community status, an orthopedic surgeon whose patients included the injured athletes at his son's high school.

The surgeon's son was 6'4"—and solid. So was his play. But far from dominating. He was a better-than-average ball handler. His shooting was fair, at best. His greatest skill was passing, and though he passed effectively, he passed up shots he should have taken. His reluctance to shoot was obvious to me. (His foul shooting was below average.) We had plenty to talk about the next time we met.

When almost all was said and the basketball season was done, I encouraged my client to seek a scholarship at an Ivy League school. His grades were very good, and his ability, I felt, was best suited to the competitive level of play in that league. "How about Dartmouth?" I said. "I know a coach up there and could introduce you." The athlete's sights were set higher. He was determined to have his net of dreams trap a bigger fish.

My story ends with this young man, after having too many fish get through the net, attending the University of North Carolina at Chapel Hill. What an ending! But some details must be provided here. Roy Williams, the Tar Heel head honcho, had coached the brother at Kansas before Williams left there to coach in Carolina. He liked the older brother, who had worked hard as a walk-on (no scholarship) and eventually performed beyond earlier assessments of his ability. The family, who had met Williams in Kansas, called him to make an appeal. The connection helped, without doubt.

Another help was the existence of a junior varsity basketball program at UNC. Very few such programs can be found across the country. But a long-standing one can be found in Chapel Hill. The boy had the will and the family and coach found the way. Patrick enrolled as a non-scholarship student and played on the J.V. team for two years. In his junior year he became a walk-on, one of the players who sees action at the very end of games in which the outcome is clearly determined. (In the Tar Heels' case, almost always a runaway victory.)

The team won the National Championship in Patrick's senior year. A happy ending, in that the boy played basketball there for four years and could now wear a championship ring. Many forces converged to bring this ending about. One of the modest forces was Patrick's modest talent. If the family's reach had initially been greater than its grasp, what they ultimately held in their collective hand was a reality that many others can only dream about. A pretty good settlement, in this case.

The end of a different young athlete's story is yet to be determined. That's because I was obligated, I thought, to try to help the boy even though he was only twelve years old. I shake my head in wonder as I write this. But I quickly offer a rationalization to explain—if not justify—my involvement with the boy.

I had spoken at a corporate gathering in Atlanta. The well-known company makes athletic equipment and apparel. The area manager contacted me and coordinated the program that day. After it was completed, we had a cup of coffee together, and he told me about his young son, who he thought was an extremely precocious athlete. Golf, football, baseball: this kid could do it all and do it well, the father said. But the dad's delivery was neither obnoxious nor imploring. He simply stated that the boy had trouble accepting any failure on the fields of play and that he, the father, wanted to help him but couldn't seem to do so. He asked if they could drive up to Brevard and have the boy talk with me.

I did all of the talking. Intimidation? Shyness? An immature uncertainness about what to say and how to say it? All of the above? I spent much time speaking about the matters the father had given me some guidance with. The kid's need to be perfect, his frustration with any mistake he made, the resultant tears—and so on. I asked many questions. His responses were made with head movements.

One of the questions I asked (his mother and father were chatting in the living room with Anita) had to do with his father's treatment of him. I told the boy that it was essential he be honest with me if any value would come of this meeting. I assured him that everything he said in the room would be held in confidence. And he assured me, eventually speaking to my point, that his dad never berated him, always encouraged him and did not set up long term goals for any kind of future in athletics. "He says he just wants me to enjoy playing, and when I get mad or cry it upsets him to see me that way."

So spoke the son, after considerable tooth-pulling.

Over the years I have gotten calls from the father asking me to talk on the phone again with his son. Each time, the boy called before school in the morning and each time assured me each time he has gotten better at managing his emotions and would try to fix the current set-back. I followed up after one particular important competition and trusted the report that he responded well to a couple of adverse circumstances.

The major thrust of this story is that there are some parents out there who 'get it.' In this case, the boy (I believe this, without ever having seen him compete) is an exceptional talent. Yet the father seems grounded. In other cases I dealt with, I encountered boys with moderate talent and parents with immoderate behavior. Many of the fathers were living vicariously through their child's talent, such as it was thought to be. Here was a sensible dad and an overly sensitive young son. Perhaps this athlete will prove to be 'the real deal.' Time will reveal all.

The final story offers a third example—and a good one, for me. Because, in this case, the parent had a sincere, appropriate and justifiable concern—and absolutely no illusions. A woman was in the supermarket checkout line, waiting her turn. She glanced at the magazine rack nearby and saw a picture of Mickey Rourke on one of the covers.

"I like him," she later told me, "So I picked up the magazine. That's when I saw a line on the side that mentioned a sport psychologist who worked with top baseball players." She purchased the magazine and read the article about the baseball guy—me. (I hope she read about Mickey Rourke first.) I received a letter from her shortly thereafter.

Articulate and direct, this letter told of a son who was an asthmatic and had difficulties in school—though he was smart—because of dyslexia. (She had no awareness of my own history with asthma.) She talked about her 15-year-old son's tendency to be a loner, his lack of social confidence, his self-image—and his love of baseball. He played. He was not a great talent, she wrote, but his enjoyment for the game, a seemingly singular enthusiasm he had, was adversely affected by his inability to execute to his capabilities on the field.

She closed her letter by saying she knew I was busy and did not know how much my fee would be. A single mother, she told me she would do whatever it took if allowed to drive up from South Carolina and have the boy spend some time with me.

I tracked down the phone number and called her. Two hours on an upcoming Saturday morning, no fee. "Just bring a cake," I said, to amuse myself. The drive, I knew, would take under four hours. "If you left real early, you could get here by ten. That would be perfect," I told her. She was excited.

They arrived a few minutes early. Anita spent the two hours in the kitchen, chatting with the mother, drinking coffee and—eating the cake she had made. (This woman was serious.) The boy and I spent the two hours in my office. A fine and sensitive young man (too sensitive, of course) answered me directly and, I felt certain, honestly. He let it all out regarding his predicament on and off the field. We spent most of our time 'off the field.'

His mom is a very intelligent and seemingly self-assured woman. A loving mother of an only child, a single parent in their home, she was aware and wary of her understandable tendency to over-protect. (I told her I had fled from such treatment when I was fifteen.)

They drove home with some energy and a renewed sense of hope for future prospects, based on strategies we had developed. The e-mail I received from the mom a few days later told of his enthusiasm to integrate these strategies into his behavior. And, the proud mother wrote, "He's doing it! I can't believe a two-hour meeting could lead to such dramatic changes."

"To his great credit," I answered.

The mother said all the right things; she was a breath of fresh air for me, who had heard enough bullshit from parents to fertilize Mars. We continue to exchange e-mails when she determines the communication to be warranted. An occasional phone call. I always advise a player (person), who is questioned by others about his apparent deficiencies, to say in response, "I'm working on it." Nick is working on it—and doing a pretty good job of it.

But I will see no more high school students—or parents, most of whom bring with them the warm and sunny climate of illusion.

13

For Want of Courage

So much of my life has been spent thinking and talking about the topic of courage that I feel compelled to write about it here. (I have written a few paragraphs about it in other books.)

The line I have quoted often to athletes is credited to one Sydney Smith, an English writer who was very quotable. "A great deal of talent is lost in this world for want of a little courage." I cannot count how many talented players I have known who, because they would not or could not muster enough mental strength—courage—in the face of adversity, had careers that were shorter and less productive than they should have been.

My interest in the subject began at an early age—because of my own deficit and a subsequent imperative for survival on the street where I lived—in the Bronx. Thanks to a father who always seemed to provide the right words at the right time and to his brother, an uncle who seemed to do better for his nieces and nephews than he could do for himself, I was able to learn—and expand and fortify my heart. My uncle took me to Stillman's Gym in Manhattan, where a boxer-friend of his taught me how to defend myself. A one-liner from Rocky Graziano, to whom I was introduced after my first lesson, provided a prevailing street philosophy. Its theme: strike before getting struck, though the wording was more colloquial. Vulgar, actually. Gratefully received.

Still, those lessons were not entirely on point, in terms of what I have tried to teach (and follow). I will clarify. The term *courage* is synonymous with bravery, will, intrepidity and fortitude. Courage is considered to be the ability to confront fear, pain, danger, risk, the unknown—and intimidation. But the distinction I have made with players has to do with *moral* courage, as opposed to *physical* courage. I have already spoken about hockey players who have what I consider to be highly developed physical courage. They face and manage their bodies' pain extremely well.

But when it comes to *moral* courage, these athletes fall along the bell-shaped curve in the same places as those competing in other sports. In the same random placement as mass man, for that matter. Because if *moral* courage means to act appropriately—rightly—in the face of external social pressures, personal embarrassment, discouragement or adversity, then hockey players and other professional athletes are in the general collective, along with Barry Blackberry, of 'typical human beings.'

That is not a compliment in my book—this book. Few people aspire to typicality, normality—mediocrity. But many are skewered in place with the other many.

One of my standard introductory questions to professional baseball players who I meet for the first time goes like this: "If I tell you that you'll be successful if you give me two things—intelligence and courage—and you tell me that you can only give me one of them, which do you think I'd ask for?"

The answer most often is "intelligence." I respond by explaining that playing the game of baseball doesn't require all that much intelligence. But it does require a greater degree of courage than "ordinary" people seem to have. Whatever 'smarts' a player may have is negated by his lack of courage. Any person who acts out of his fears forfeits whatever intelligence he possesses, since that individual behaves emotionally, rather than rationally.

People often dismiss their flaws by rationalizing them. "I'm only human," is a declaration I heard more than a few times from people who are trying to defend their weak behavior to me. (Did they think the alternate behavior I suggested required them to be superhuman?) My responses were not sympathetic.

The Latin *cor* means "heart." To have courage is to have 'heart.' That term is heard often enough around ballparks and corporate offices. To many, it implies fearlessness. But that isn't the point of courage. To have courage is to act bravely *in spite* of the existence of fear. During my association with pitcher Dennis Eckersley, I witnessed daily acts of courage on the part of the Hall-of-Famer. Here was a pitcher—a man—who fought and won the battle against alcoholism, and who announced to the world that he was terrified of failure. Of public humiliation. Yet he had to confront it on a regular basis as the 'closer' for the Oakland Athletics, a team that went to three consecutive World Series during Eckersley's All-Star, MVP and Cy Young Award tenure.

The strategy Dennis was required to employ was clear to him. Essentially, it was 'If I don't want to fail, then rather than acting out what I *feel*, I'll act out what I *know* will help me succeed.' Courage was required, and courage was shown. He was a consistently aggressive performer. And courage was evident in that consistency, which he expressed irrespective of circumstance. As a recovered alcoholic, Eck recognized that it is one's self a person abandons when he acts cowardly.

The American Heritage Dictionary defines courage as "the state of mind or spirit that enables one to face danger with self-possession, confidence and resolution." I would argue that 'confidence' is not a prerequisite of courage. It is more often an end, than a mean. When I was confident, I did not need courage. I was spurred to act by that confidence. But when I lacked confidence, a different stimulus was required. That spur was the courage of confrontation. When I confronted a bully on a Bronx street, I was sure of one thing: I was going to get my ass kicked. But courage allowed me to be aggressive and implement Graziano's strategy, despite the absence of confidence.

I was able to master many other difficulties I have faced without an initial confidence in a favorable outcome—or even in the certainty that I would *behave* appropriately. But, by the blood, I tried. Whatever Yoda says about that word, I respect the attempt as much (more?) as the result.

One of my points of emphasis when talking to a player about this topic is that courage is inherent *in the brave act itself.* (I prefer the term, 'appropriate act.') The *resolve* is more essential to courage than the confidence, which usually comes as a *result* of behaving with "self-possession . . . and resolution." As a sickly young boy, I gained self-confidence after appropriate action, no matter what the outcome might have been. Confronting that neighborhood bully didn't win me pugilistic points, but it did win self-respect—and respect from the bully, who did not enjoy being stood up to (and whacked), and who lost interest in me thereafter.

Physical "danger" is not my point, as I think I have made clear. Stories of seemingly monumental physical heroism leave readers impressed, yet detached from the realities of the hero and his circumstance. But people are very much attached to their own daily circumstances—to their own struggles and needs. And they are just as attached to their frustration and/or sense of failure, when the external world seems to be controlling their internal world. When they can't act out the appropriate behaviors they would wish to act out, "for want of a little courage."

A few years ago, a player came to Brevard and spent two days with me. In the course of our talks, he revealed a "problem" he was "really struggling with." He told me he felt diminished (rightly so, I said after he finished his explanation) by his handling ("non-handling," I corrected) of the situation. The situation was this: "My wife and I are building a new house (in California). The landscaper is screwing me. His bill is ridiculously high—and the work he's done was half-assed."

I asked if he had paid the bill. "Not yet," he answered, to my relief.

"Good. Now you can (will!) confront the guy and tell him what you told me," I said. "You might choose to change your language. You might not," I said, as an afterthought. "Make the judgment of what style would be most effective with this particular guy. I mean, present it so as to most likely accomplish what you want to accomplish."

Then I asked a hypothetical question. "Suppose you and I were sitting at a bar, and a guy came up to me and talked trash about me being a bald-headed old man who should find his walker and get the hell home. And he took me by the arm to encourage that me to do so. What would you do?"

The answer came before my lips closed. "I'd beat the shit out of him."

My next remark: "And you won't confront your landscaper about an injustice done to you?" I let the rhetorical question rest for a moment. Then I said that if he couldn't confront this issue, he had wasted his time flying all the way from California to see me. "You're being an enabler," I told him, "without guts enough to tell the truth as you believe it to be. This guy works for you. *You're* the boss." The remark startled him.

"You're thinking he's controlling me," he said.

"He is," I responded, "Until you do something to prove otherwise."

I told him I'd give him a week (after he arrived home) to "face up." A call to me was part of the assignment. Four days later, the deed was done. He had prepared himself to fight a fierce and ruthless life battle, only to have the enemy surrender at the first show of the opposition's weaponry. I did not say, "I told you so," even though I had said the possibility was great that this would happen. Of course, that possibility had never resided in his mind.

A major league under-achiever—on and off the field—came for a visit. As per the schedule set for such visits, Anita makes dinner the first night, and we enjoy the homey atmosphere with discussions of family (baby pictures produced by the player, at Anita's insistence) and trivialities. The second night, we go out for dinner.

This player, as is the case with so many others, is kind, polite, and socially 'careful,' meaning he wants to call as little attention to himself as possible. In terms of what he says—what he *used to* say—I was reminded of a line I wrote to a former student many years ago, while she was away at college. Aeschylus wrote it first (*Prometheus Bound*): "There is no sickness worse / for me than words that to be kind must lie." What I pointed out to my former English student was that 'being kind' is often the more palatable term for being timid. It is not kind, I wrote her, to be permissive at your own expense. To be manipulated and controlled.

It may be kind to lie when you say a friend looks attractive in her new dress (depending on circumstance, it may *not* be), but it is not kind to say you feel no pain from the dagger the 'friend' has put in your heart. A hurtful public remark about you that caused great embarrassment, for example.

So—Anita, the player and I were eating out on the second night at a local Chinese restaurant. The ideas expressed above had been discussed earlier in the day. He had provided specific examples of his lies and "cowardly acts to avoid confrontation," as he aptly put it. Psyche-sustaining behavior, I called it.

The waitress greeted us as we placed ourselves in the booth, putting three glasses of water on the table and departing to get menus. Our companion looked at his water glass. A small foreign object was floating around in there. The waitress returned and placed the menus in front of us. The player spoke: "Excuse me, Miss. There's something in my water. Could I have another glass, please?"

The waitress apologized profusely, picked up the glass and left. The player, sitting next to me, turned his head and said, "Harv, it's working!" A major achievement? Eight years removed, he remains quite proud of (and amused by) that recollection.

One last story about this guy. It is a favorite of mine. The player went back home—to Miami. We followed up on the phone, part of the 'program.' During one call, he excitedly told me about an occurrence the previous day. His wife was having trouble with her car and had to drop it off at the dealership for repair. Their plan called for Ralph (my pseudonym for him) to follow her in his car and take her back home with him. He was driving a convertible with the top down. At a red light, the wife was stopped in the right lane. She was first in a line of cars waiting behind her for the light to change.

Ralph was the second car in the left lane, so he was diagonally behind her. The wife was distracted, lost in thought or reverie, when the red turned to green. Ralph's wife sat there "just for a few seconds," he reported to me. But they were a few seconds too many for the guy in the car behind her. He blew his horn in an extended blare.

A beautiful fall day in Florida. Ralph with his car's top down, the guy to his right with his window down, pumping one hand in the air in a whassamatter-widyou? gesture, as the other maintained the horn blast. This became immediately disconcerting to Ralph, the fineness of day being subsumed with his wife's becoming the object of some bozo's impatient, impolite intolerance.

Ralph continued his telephone report to me. "So I said to myself: What would Harvey do now?" I waited with great interest as he paused for effect. "And I yelled at the guy, 'Fuck you!'"

"Ralph," I aid, controlling hysteria. "Do you really think I'd say that? I mean, that's like dropping an atom bomb on an ant."

"Well, maybe it was too aggressive, but I couldn't let him get away with that shit after all we had talked about."

I told him I understood. "If you drop a pendulum from one side, it doesn't stop in the middle. It swings to the other extreme. Ralph, I hope it settles in the middle soon." It did, as his future behavior and success have indicated.

In earlier years, when I picked players up at the Phoenix airport, the first question I asked them referred to a hypothetical setting. "You're really hungry and you decide to go to a fine restaurant. You order a favorite dish from the menu and look forward to the meal with great anticipation. It's set before you. You put the first forkful into your mouth: the food is not hot. Maybe it's even cold. What do you do?"

A question asked years ago, and I did not keep an accurate count of where responses fell on the either/or scale. But with a reluctance to exaggerate, I will say that six or seven out of ten who were asked that question responded, "I'd eat it." It did not surprise me, since, as I had said to Jim Abbott, "That's why you're here."

One very interesting variation. A player thought about the question for an extended moment, then said, "I'd send it back—unless I saw the waitress give me a dirty look. Then I'd say, 'Oh, that's all right,' and eat it."

I pointed out to the six or seven that the waitress wanted to please them; she wanted a good tip. "She's there to serve and please you," I told them. "There isn't even a logical reason to be intimidated by her. She'll say, 'Oh, I'm sorry sir; I'll have the cook get it nice and hot.' Or something like that. Now, the chef might be unhappy and spit in your plate, but that's unlikely."

My intent is to define and address the seemingly small acts of courage that are 'in want' in the private and compelling world of 'Everyman's' psyche. It's about perceived, as well as real, discomfort, dysfunction and 'danger' in social settings, in the workplace and in family life. Any environment, actually, in which an individual moves and settles. Or avoids.

Avoids, because his or her state of mind or spirit is not up to it. So a pitcher wishes to avoid contact of his pitch with the hitter's bat, or his neighbor wants to avoid contact and conflict with his auto mechanic. Courage is wanting. As it is when a friend avoids confrontation with another friend, who is being hurtful or damaging to himself or his family members; when a person submissively eats that cold food. "It doesn't matter," he rationalizes. Or when a co-worker's back-stabbing is discovered and the wounded party talks to everyone about it except the knife-wielder; when a parent is permissive because he or she is afraid to lose a child's love. Courage is wanting. "All goes if courage goes," J.M. Barrie wrote.

It was Ben Franklin who said, "Without justice, courage is weak." Conversely, without courage, justice can't be well served. Justice within circumstance, justice within self. The opposing athlete, the landscaper, the plumber, the boss, the subordinate, the colleague, the friend, the son or daughter, the spouse will be appropriately communicated with in difficult circumstances *only* when and if the individual acts courageously upon self-evident truths.

Our attempts to avoid confrontation are focused on fear. "Fear itself" becomes the biggest problem. FDR said so in his first inaugural address a couple of years before I was born. It was repeated for my benefit many times after my infancy by a father who sensed my early experiences and over-protective treatment by his spouse might produce a 'courage-challenged' son. His concern was justified and, for a time, prophetic. Early on, I found that whatever I tried to avoid was around the corner waiting for me.

Pitcher Bob Welch used to imitate me (I've told this many, many times) by saying, "If you told Harvey you just killed somebody, he'd say, 'What are we going to do about it?'" Well, he was probably right. I wouldn't pull my hair out (what's left); I wouldn't scream in horror. I'd want to know if he would turn himself in, kill himself, run away and hide or kill someone else. I would want to know what he was *inclined* to "do about it," and help him determine the appropriate thing to do.

That is part of the first questions I ask myself, which are "What *can* I do?" and "What is the *right thing* to do?" The courage is not in the asking, of course. It is in the doing. Fear has an emotional basis, whereas a plan or strategy has a rational one. It gets back to what players claim about me: "He doesn't care about your feelings; he cares about your actions." (Tim Belcher) When I integrate a rational, aggressive plan into a behavioral approach to an issue or circumstance, I am able to pre-empt any fear I might have. As I tell players constantly, "Being afraid can be understood, forgiven—accepted. Acting cowardly cannot."

My behavior is entirely within my control. I do not measure my courage against the behavior of others. I measure it against the degree of fear or reluctance to confront what I perceive to be unpleasant, uncomfortable, threatening or dangerous. The more I avoided these weaknesses as a youth, the more the traits were reinforced. I was worn out at a very early age and decided that the struggle for a better existence was not nearly as psychologically draining as the giving in had been. The fighting was, as I've said, its own reward. Victory was a dividend of delight. Victories mounted, albeit slowly.

Here, I am reminded of a chat I had with Greg Maddux, the future Hall of Fame pitcher. We stood together on a field years ago reviewing our relationship. He confessed that my early compliments to him for saying all the right things to the media were often undeserved. He said he didn't always do what he said. "And now?" I asked.

His answer was, "It's fucking scary; I can't do the wrong thing any more."

Brainwashing. He scrubbed his fears and reluctances away. It was an ordeal, surely. But it became an acquired instinct. Second nature, as it is often called. We're all capable of the acquisition of courage, if we were not blessed with the genetic predisposition for it. Habits cling. Maddux had shed yesterday's uncomfortable garment and what he now wore, would be worn again and again. The habit of efficacy was his suit; the habit of courage was the undergarment. We can all purchase the same attire. The price is persistence.

Changing the metaphor, my own young mind built a refuge from the world of social intimidation. It became a fortress with age. The value and benefit of appropriate behavior has taken me into myself and beyond myself at the same time. It is both selfish and selfless. (More on that in the following chapter.)

One last thought, related to words I posted above the blackboard in my classroom years ago: "Present fears are less than horrible imaginings." Shakespeare knew that what was real and right in front of our faces was not as debilitating to our psyches as what we conjured up about awful future possibilities. The exhaustion of giving in was palpable when I was a boy. But I thank the fates that I never was afraid of anything that *might* happen. (OK, once, I remember now, when I was seven years old.) I was busy enough trying to navigate through the rough waters of my actual existence. Many I have met are not so blessed.

Is being a slave of imagination worse than being a slave to reality? The question reminds me of the gangster movie I saw as a kid. The bad guy has the good guy at his mercy. He is going to shoot him, no question about that. But he asks the victim-to-be, "How do you want it, in the belly or in the back?" I would guess that some people I know would have answered, "Both."

I value my freedom greatly, and being socially enslaved is out of my life-equation. But I know I do not have freedom from all conditions. Yet, as Viktor Frankl pointed out in a book that was very important to me (*Man's Search for Meaning*), I do have "freedom to take a stand toward conditions." The potential to confront those conditions with courage and whatever intelligence I have. If I do so, I will never be a slave to the misery of fear. With courage, I will be free.

14

The Art of Selfishness

The previous chapter has led me to revisit another topic I am engaged with very often in my work. It usually becomes a language issue; and semanti-therapy plays a big role in my intervention. People understand me—and themselves—according to the words we use and the definitions attached to them.

The conventional lexicon has made 'selfishness' a dirty word. It suggests that a selfish man lives by himself and for himself. That kind of definition is limited in scope and limiting in application. Major league baseball play-ers understand that. "In baseball," they say, "you can be selfish and still help the team." By this they mean: 'Take care of your own stuff and you'll be contributing to the good of those around you.' Or words to that effect. What I say is: "If you don't know how to take care of yourself, you'll prob-ably not be able to take care of others."

I have tried to tell players that a person who isn't self-aware is a person who can't profoundly understand his world and the people in it. Introspec-tion is an initial step but, as Goethe suggests, not a final one: "Self-knowl-edge is best learned, not by contemplation, but action."

First, we must know ourselves; know what *we* believe; know what to do and when and how to do it. I tell people to employ "dutiful action" for themselves. Speaking with them on a daily basis—athletes and non-athletes—I can visualize some of their heads on swivels, looking around, watching others. They're either keying off them so as to know how to act, or they're disparaging them. Trying to diminish others becomes a primary activity. A not-so-quiet desperation.

"I know, I know." Those are the two words I too frequently hear when I point out behaviors of that sort to players. As I have said before, it is not an adequate response. We all have to get beyond the knowing, to the doing. To action beyond acknowledgement.

Self-awareness, self-trust, self-control and all the other 'self's' that help create self-efficacy come under the umbrella of *appropriate selfishness*. So I offer no apology for being selfish. Most who believe the term 'selfishness' to have a negative connotation probably haven't considered or understood the word's extensional meaning. Perhaps they themselves have no goals beyond 'being nice.'

Many athletes complain to me about their being "too soft" during competition. They're not happy with themselves as competitors (to begin with). One major league pitcher recently expressed such unhappiness to me. "Every time I screw up in a game, all my focus is on what the manager is thinking about me." He went on, "All I can think about is pleasing the guy." The player was obviously distracted from his task; he was fearful and frustrated. And ineffective. His manager was displeased. "I'm tired of being a nice guy and worrying about others," the player said to me.

"Good," I responded. "You're ready to be selfish."

It was more than twenty years ago when a pitcher who had lost 16 games with two different teams the previous season came to my hotel room during spring training. We were both then with the Oakland Athletics. He was—and still is—one of the finest gentlemen I've ever come across. That evening in 1988, I told him that his disposition off the field was irrelevant to me. His performance persona wasn't working for him, and that was our immediate concern. I railed on about developing a "warrior mentality" when pitching. "Your nice-guy act isn't cutting it in competition," I said.

"You don't want me to be a nice guy?" he shouted with some resentment. "OK, then teach me how to be an asshole!"

I smiled. "A gentleman is someone who's sensitive to the needs of others," I explained, over-simplifying for the sake of expediency (wanting to get to *his* word—and my definition of it). "An asshole, as you put it, is someone who is *insensitive* to the needs of others." *That's* what you've got to be when you compete—insensitive to the crowd, to the media, to the manager, to the opposing dugout—the score, your statistics. . ."

He stopped me. "Enough," he said. "I get it."

He was later 'to get' a lecture from me about being "too much of a gentleman off the field, as well." I waited for him to show he had understood the first message before I delivered what I thought to be the more difficult one. Eventually, he was ready to hear it. To understand and to act out "the right behavior, rather than the easy behavior."

Too many 'nice guys' submit to the very questionable motives of others, in order to avoid conflict. The aim of 'Mr. Nice Guy' is to ingratiate himself to others. His payoff is the illusion of safety and security. He seeks comfort. He avoids justified confrontation or conflict. (Or intense competition.) Such a person chooses to yield and retreat with ease, comforted by the fact that he didn't have to face a mental challenge, a difficult interpersonal confrontation. Unable to muster the necessary courage, he denies his failure and is comforted by the perceived safety of acquiescence. ("Caving-in," is one of the terms used term in the world of sport.)

But at another level of consciousness, the nice-guy-retreat produces a recurring sense of danger and discomfort—to go along with a growing sense of inferiority. One of his aims during competition is to do nothing to upset the opposition and to maintain the 'Nice Guy' image. The same behavior can be seen in offices, at business gatherings and dinner parties.

These folks may declare themselves to be nice people, but being fearful and foolish is not synonymous with being nice. Many protest to me that their behavior is nobly selfless. Please. They're serving selves that have no vitality and, therefore, no vital purpose. That's not really so nice, after all.

One of my less pleasant tasks over the years was to address a family issue with a particular major league player. In the player's hotel room in Detroit, I had the *audacity* (his word) to criticize his behavior strongly (and support his wife's point of view). I remarked on what I considered his emotional immaturity. He countered vehemently, arms flailing as he provided his reasons. I told him that his 'supporting' major and minor premises, on which he based his self- justification was "pig-logic."

"You're not a nice guy," he shouted. He didn't speak to me for two years.

My 'not-niceness' (honesty and assertiveness) caused discomfort; his niceness (self-gratification and denial) had caused harm. He didn't understand the difference between my selfishness and his.

As counterpoint to that incident was a situation in which I was asked by a major league coach, a colleague, to speak with his wife. She wanted to have counseling in order to resolve a couple of issues about herself. Her husband had recommended she call me.

We met. She was pleased with the exchange and wanted to follow up. I suggested she call a local counselor I knew, one who practiced close to her home. She knew I traveled in my job and could only occasionally have meetings with her.

She followed my advice. Months later, her husband asked me to call her, which I did. She wasn't comfortable with the counselor, she told me. I asked her why this was so.

"He's too nice," she answered.

"What do you mean?" I asked.

"I can't trust him to tell me what I need to hear about myself," she said.

We're good for ourselves when we're true to ourselves. And we're good for others when we are as true—when we act on our understanding of what we know to be right. When we are selfish in the right way. Not self-indulgent. Not fake. Not fearful. Not "too nice" or "just plain nice"—those agendas being to please or placate.

My paying attention to my own needs and being attentive to the needs of others are *not* mutually exclusive. My task is to strike an effective balance. That requires persistence and sensitivity, compassion and courage. I hope I have managed to strike that balance. I am reminded of the words of Paul West: "Those who bite the bullet need not eat the gun."

Selfishness which serves someone at the expense of someone else is deplorable. I don't advocate or encourage people to be 'users.' The 'not-so-nice guy' is not a person who pursues his own good, but a guy who harms or neglects others.

On the playing field, he is the team member who focuses on his own interests exclusively. His statistics mean more to him than the team's success. He's happy when he has a good game, despite the team's loss. He surrounds himself with people who have the same attitude.

The self-absorbed and self-indulged are corrupted by the company they keep. Their selfishness is not only in living as they wish to live, but in asking or expecting others to live the same way. In seeking to benefit only himself, 'Mr. Really-Not-Nice Guy' often employs mean-spirited tactics that do harm to others. These acts are transparent—but the actor usually gets away with his act, because 'nice guys' turn the other way—resenting them, complaining about them, doing nothing about them.

It takes some strength of character to hold others accountable for doing the right thing. People in sport and business arenas constantly look for such leaders. (Everywhere but in the mirror?)

Players have asked me, "Who do you tell your stuff to?" I respond with standard flippant answers, essentially telling them I know how to take care of my own 'stuff.' They trust it, giving me more credit than I probably deserve. I'm trying to project to them what I'd like them to project to others. I encourage them to work at self-efficacy, rather than self-absorption. To be attentive to self, while not being self-indulgent. Self-indulgence is most obvious in the world of the professional athlete. It can also be found in society at-large without that much effort. Advertisers are well aware of people's potential for it.

'Mr. Really-Good Guy' develops an ability to heal himself. He learns to take care of himself in a manner that encourages him to act out the behaviors appropriate to circumstance. He learns to make tough decisions. To trust himself. He's not obsessed with pleasing others.

I often offer 'pleasers' Robert Frost's thought: "It's important to have the right enemies." Explaining the poet's words, I say, "I don't want everyone to like me. If jerks like me I'm doing something wrong." It may be a philosophical stretch, but the point is that I know if I act out my best instincts, good people will not be displeased with me.

We don't need to be physicians to heal ourselves. We just need to be selfish in the right way.

Self-absorption for the purpose of self-discovery may be well intentioned, but it can also be self-defeating. Counter-productive, at least. Self-interest to the extreme is probably responsible for the constant stream of self-help books on the best-seller list each week. I said this earlier in the book. Readers continually seek easy answers in self-help books that essentially offer similar messages. My thoughts on the matter: 1) The readers learned the answers long ago; 2) Reading doesn't get the job done.

Finally, I wish to summarize my personal attempts at the art of selfishness. An initial understanding was prerequisite, if I was to be artful, rather than artless: What is good for me must not hurt others. At the same time, when occasionally presented by daunting choices, following another credo—'do no unnecessary harm"—I have seen my painful choices lead to painful results for others. To butcher a moral from an Aesop fable: A stroke for some is a kick in the pants for others, albeit a necessary kick.

I also believe that my only duty is to do as much as I can as well as I can. I try to be realistic and rational, rather than urgent and emotional. I give myself self time to reflect, develop and decide, because I believe that change is a process that should not cater to the demands a clock.

Over the years, I have tried to recognize my abilities and strengths and foster them, rather than abandoning them as I addressed weaknesses and patterns I wished to change. The challenge of being true to what I care about and love has been worth the effort, though I have not always been successful. It has been important to me, even more so as I've grown older, to devote myself to those people and ideas I choose to value greatly—and to be loyal and dedicated to them.

A desire for the comfort that comes from pleasing others is self-inhibiting and/or self-diminishing. I don't do it. I accept my genes, but have not believed myself to be a victim of them—except when I surrendered to that easy excuse. That hasn't happened since my days of adolescent immaturity.

I hope I have developed and maintained a personal and professional standard. I know I have fortified myself against compromises that result from trying to placate people who might be envious of whatever achievements I might have managed.

The right of choice is mine. This I recognized many years ago. Many years ago. Some choices have been difficult and/or unpleasant. To forfeit a right choice "for want of courage" is to forfeit my freedom.

Finally, I have worked hard at refusing generalizations, labels, false slogans, emotionally-loaded language and stereotypes. I have been very careful about recognizing the difference between symbol and substance. Now, as Greg Maddux would say (*sans* swearing), 'I can't do it wrong anymore.'

I'm hearing myself repeating what I've already written. Maybe it's because these words come out of my mouth on a daily basis. Still, I'm getting bored. (Probably, I'm not the only one.) And though I may even have sounded didactic in this chapter (not before?), I realize it's because, in a book about myself, I want very much to represent that self as definitively as possible.

That's being selfish, I guess.

15

Funnyball

"Methinks he doth protest too much." That was the first title I had in mind for this chapter. To be absolutely literal, Hamlet's mother said, "The lady doth protest too much, methinks." Gertrude offered her view as she watched a play (devised by Hamlet to make her squirm a little. . .) about a man who killed his brother and married the widow—essentially what just happened in her own life, she being the widow. In the play, the woman defended herself against accepting responsibility for her unsavory actions (marrying her dead husband's brother). Gertrude was basically saying the character would be a lot more believable if she weren't so excessively vocal about her innocence. In other words, the more you try to talk your way out of something you've done, the less people are likely to believe you.

My chapter has to do with a 'he,' not a 'she.' And, though I have taken some liberty with Shakespeare, I believe I am to be taken literally about all else written in these pages. Mecertainlythinks the 'he' hath protested much too much.

But let me start at the proper place: the beginning, where a funny thing happened on the way to . . . the kitchen. My phone rang. It was a Hollywood director. She wanted me to appear in a movie. (I must be believed here, because I promised to be literal—truthful.) I, myself, thought it was a joke, some smart-ass player's wife messing with me. Not so. I also thought (my mind working rapidly under the pressure of Hollywood's call) of the magazine article that had come out months before, the writer rather exaggerating, I thought, my un-Hollywood physiognomy. "She couldn't have seen that." That was my thought.

Whatever the case, I told her I did not think I was interested in her offer. Then she told me about the film—and I *knew* I wasn't interested. She said she was directing a film based on the book *Moneyball*, which had hit the non-fiction bestseller list shortly after publication in 2003. How the hell could they make a movie about that book? I asked the director that question. I might have had my own answer had I read the book. (I'd made a point of *not* reading it, though enough people had told me more than enough about it.) But the director filled me in.

She asked if I had seen the film, *Reds*. I said I had, though I would be hard pressed to provide the plot for her. That didn't matter, she told me. "Remember all the people who offered commentary, interrupting the plot throughout?" she asked.

"The talking heads?" I said.

"Yes. We have a number of people lined up to do that, and we want you to be one of them."

I then remembered the film *Sweet and Lowdown*, in which that device was used. Woody Allen, Nat Hentof and others offered commentary that was interspersed throughout the film. Would I be allowed to write my own lines? I was titillated by the thought.

"I'm not interested," I told her. "I have a strong bias against the subject of the movie—of the book. A very negative feeling." She told me that had no bearing on my inclusion and tried to persuade me further, but I did not yield.

The next day, the assistant director, a young man, by the sound of his voice, tried a different approach: more palsy, laid-back, casual. Cool. I engaged this pleasant fellow for a few minutes before we ended the conversation. He had climbed the tree, but he didn't come down with any fruit. I was determined not to get involved in this project, one that I now understood—in a funny way—was serious.

The following day, I received an e-mail from one of the secretaries in our California office. She wrote that the film's producer had called her, left his phone number and told her, "Harvey said he wants to talk to me." I e-mailed back, saying I had never indicated any such thing—to anyone. She, in turn, answered my message with these words: "I just *knew* he was lying. I shouldn't have bothered you." I assured her it was not a bother. "Funny, actually."

When I told all this to my daughter, Melissa, she was adamant, telling me that Hollywood people were tenacious and obnoxious. "They think everyone gives in to them." (Was I being praised or warned?) My son, Dan, pretended to be disappointed. "Maybe I could have gotten a cameo role," he said. (Did he think I would be the co-star with Brad Pitt. "Yes, Brad Pitt," I told him, trying to suspend his disbelief.)

So endeth thoughts of glitz and glitter, but Hollywood's beck and call did provoke me to Google a curiosity stimulated by the exchanges. There I found a couple of excerpts from *Moneyball*, one of which held my interest.

Billy Beane, is the General Manager and minority owner of the Oakland Athletics. His pronouncements and well-promulgated—often maligned—philosophy of running a small-market team and playing a big-time winning game on the field elevated him to prominence and, some say, to arrogance. (Billy Bashers are amused and/or put off by his video game for aspiring General Managers.) But it is easier to judge than to perform. (I'll attempt to confine my own 'judgments' to a few specific remarks Billy provided for the book's. Not yet, though.)

A former New York Mets number one pick in the 1980 amateur draft, Billy Beane, never reached the great potential others had seen in him. An outfielder with all the skills scouts look for, he struggled. The Mets traded him to Minnesota in 1986; Minnesota traded him to Detroit in 1988; he came to Oakland as a free agent in 1989. It was then that I first met him. We met often in spring training. Billy was highly intelligent, reflective and a good listener. Our relationship was—and remained, for as long as we communicated with each other—cordial and friendly. He was (and still is, I would guess) a bibliophile. He was an active participant and contributor during these talks, more enthusiastic about books and family than about self—and performance issues.

Michael Lewis, the writer of *Moneyball*, wrote that people in baseball thought that "what Billy really needed was a shrink." He makes much of Billy's post at-bat emotional displays, saying that he "was one of the most efficient destroyers of baseball equipment his teammates had ever seen." I had seen many who could compete, but certainly that lack of control warranted attention, and we attended to it.

Lewis further stated that "Beane struggled (as a young Mets player) and unaccustomed to failure, he was unable to make the adjustments necessary when playing tougher competition."

When Lewis called me (2001? 2002?), he asked me for my take on Billy, the player. He wrote that I believed Billy had played hide-and-seek with his baseball demons and that baseball had won that game. He presented a remark which, though I had strong empirical evidence to support it, I had made to 'cover Billy's back.' I told Lewis about many young players like Billy, saying that organizations more-than-occasionally mishandle some of their "highly-talented player(s) who have trouble with failure." Such precocious talents, I went on, were not skilled at developing coping mechanisms, because they never had any previous failure to cope with.

Methinks that was supportive and, perhaps, a bit insightful for lay readers.

Billy thought ("felt" would be more accurate) otherwise, apparently. He offered Lewis (who had undoubtedly apprised him of my words) what the author thought was "a radically different" view of himself. Lewis wrote: "He (Billy) thought it was bullshit to say that his character—or more exactly—his emotional predisposition—might be changed. . . . All these attempts to manipulate his psyche he regarded as so much crap."

Methinks this was neither done, nor said. Selective memory? Whatever one chooses to call it, I call bullshit on Billy's response. That quote from Lewis is filled with telling terms. One of them missed my funny bone: "manipulate." It's a dirty word in my professional (and personal) dictionary.

Does Billy think (feel) that people cannot change? That they are victims of an irreversible "emotional predisposition?" Perhaps he thought that he couldn't change. He was surely wrong on that one, since the change in his behavior from then to now palpable, as many (all?) I have spoken with over the years (a few still close with him) attest.

Billy continued on a slippery slope. "Sports psychologists are a crutch. An excuse for why you are doing it rather than a solution. If somebody needs them, there is a weakness in them that will prevent them from succeeding. It's not a character flaw; it's just a character flaw in baseball. It (Billy's failure) wasn't anyone's fault. I just didn't have it in me."

"A crutch"? Billy employed what is called in semantic circles a dysphemism, which *suggested* the most disagreeable aspect of a point he wished to establish, rather than using the word itself. That word is 'dependency'—and Billy knew damn well, or should have, that a healthy independence is what I ask each athlete to strive for as a goal.

Excuses? (Youthinks projection here, Sigmund?) I will take the liberty of quoting myself, from the book I wrote for coaches: "To make an excuse is to transfer responsibility. We try to teach our athletes to be responsible. . . . An excuse engenders weakness (funny I should say this), rather than courage. The courage of *honest introspection* (my emphasis here) is a required first step toward *changing* (more of my emphasis, get it?) of negative, ingrained habits. . . . Awareness is the first step to change. If no one else tells a person about his tendency, the person is left with himself as his sole resource."

I concluded by saying that athletes don't *get* the power, they "take it." It must be an active pursuit. Many people are inclined to be passive. Others, of course, are submissive, giving in to a change they do not believe is possible—or denying a deficiency they do not admit exists.

Methinks a few more things. If this were a formal debate, I would hardly be able to keep my pencil off my yellow pad as Billy spoke. But I will control computer-fingers, because, funny thing, I trust that the force and emotionally loaded language of Billy's reaction provide plenty of evidence as to an underlying agenda.

I am sounding like a prosecutor. If I truly was one, I would call a few former clients up to the witness stand—MVP's, Cy Young winners, current and future Hall-of-Famers. On second thought ("after deliberation," would be the proper professional way of expressing myself), I would just offer them as Exhibits A through Z—evidence of successful players

I admire because of their achievements after professional, performance-related intervention.

If Billy took the stand and went on about his view that players who seek counsel are weak, Jack Clark, Todd Stottlemyre, Jason Varitek and a couple of others I could name would probably jump the rail and punch his dim lights out for the suggestion.

But I am not in a courtroom and, alas, I will not be in a film. This is only a little chapter in a little book of no real consequence.

Moneyball is a big book with, it seems, a big movie to be based on it. In the book, Lewis said of Billy the baseball player, "Somehow the game had shrunk him." Perhaps Billy's post-player career gives further evidence of some form of shrinkage.

Questioned during an early year in his general-managership, Billy said his organization didn't need a sport psychologist because he didn't sign players with such a need. (So there really were such players? An indication that his memory, at least, has shrunk over the years.)

If my own memory serves me, I remember receiving telephone calls in recent years from at least a dozen individuals who were wearing Oakland uniforms at the time of their call. Coaches included. I had a lunch meeting, as per a request, with one of his managers while I was still traveling on the road. These people must have slipped through Billy's psychological security screen before they were brought onboard.

Flashback (Maybe I *am* Hollywood material): To the amazement of Sandy Alderson, who hired him, Billy became a scout for the A's immediately after he quit playing. Sandy told Lewis, "I didn't think then there was a risk in making him an advance scout, because I didn't think an advance scout did anything." But Billy did do something, growing on the job and providing valuable information for Tony LaRussa and his staff.

Billy and I maintained our relationship in those days. He would speak excitedly about a good book he had read and always talked proudly and lovingly about his young daughter and happily about family life, in general.

Daniel Lewis: "By 1995, Alderson had created a new baseball corporate culture around a single baseball statistic: the on-base percentage." Sandy had Karl Kuehl implement the philosophy in the minor league system. Some have accused Billy Beane of co-opting the credit for much Sandy Alderson's creativity and philosophy. I will stick to what I know. The original implementation proceeded Billy's tenure as GM. I remember, because I was there.

Sandy remembered that Billy's job as his assistant, wrote Lewis, "was to go out and find undervalued minor league players. And then he handed Billy a pamphlet he'd commissioned. . ." Billy followed Sandy's priorities for the recruitment of young players. He introduced Billy to Bill James, the now famous statistical guru whose formulas are elaborated in *Moneyball*.

My own pursuits have led me to disabuse myself of any statistical inclination I might have had and take a more holistic view of players and their performance. I'm funny that way. I tend to believe what some guy said in the early 1900's, about using statistics in the same manner a drunken man uses lamp-posts: for support, rather than illumination. But that is a bias: I work with real people (they too can be misleading, I know), not with numbers.

Still, Sandy was a man before his time (he had the courage to hire me, after all) and Billy was the man after Sandy in Oakland. Funny (if not surprising), Sandy's view of sport psychology was not incorporated in the plan Billy adopted (or co-opted) and further developed.

Sandy had told *GQ* that after I left the A's, he did not replace me because he believed there was not a need at the time; what I had said and done ran through the organization, he said. "All of the players and coaches and staff he touched over the years . . . had become imbued with his philosophy and approach to the game. They have become Harvey's disciples."

Billy included? A funny question, depending on when it is asked.

He became an administrative assistant to Sandy in 1994, the year I left. I no longer ran into Billy, and I believe our phone contact i.e. relationship ended then. When Sandy left Oakland to take a position in the Commissioner's office in 1998, Billy was named General Manager. His reputation as a sabermetric savant became established, if not always appreciated, mostly by many old-school baseball lifers. One told me it was not the philosophy he took issue with, but the philosopher. But personal evaluations can be based on anything from projection to jealousy. Then again, it can also be provoked.

Billy's marriage subsequently failed. He told Lewis that his wife left him, "because she was unnerved by (his) intensity." I am here reminded of a conversation I had with old friends who visited us recently. We were rehashing our past experiences, which included our hirings as rookie teachers in Valley Stream, New York. I told my friends about my interview with the District Superintendent. At its conclusion, he asked me what me greatest weakness was. (Where to start?! I'd be damned if I'd tell him the truth and blow the possibility of a job.) I 'confessed' that my enthusiasm—my intensity—was so great that I sometimes got carried away. (The interviewer was not "unnerved;" I was hired.) Bullshit works—sometimes.

The claim Billy made to Lewis was that baseball marriages are *most* (my emphasis) vulnerable when a player retires. "They end when the career ends," the General Manager generalized, very much immersed in his current baseball career. Funny stuff, that. Contrary to my experience with retired players.

Theorists can shout and argue about Billy's low-budget, small market approach to winning baseball. They say the A's, though they have appeared in post-season play during Billy's tenure, have never won a championship, as they had in the past. The debate has died down since the book was first published.

But now the movie. I received a number of calls, a couple from people who will appear in the film. One was hired to be the technical director. These men told me that the movie will be less flattering than the book. "I know at least one guy who's going to hammer Billy," said one. Payback? That guy is a former on-field staff member, and Billy's reputation for post-game (and pre-game, for that matter) enraged soliloquies aimed at his staff has been well established in the industry. His hammer came down in the form of accusations and ultimatums. "He thinks he's General Patton," one former coach complained to me.

I do not wish to wield a hammer (or a pearl-handled pistol). But I was certainly tempted when I read his remarks suggesting that players become dependent on sport psychologists—on me, by insinuation. My agenda has always been—and immediately made clear to players—that independence is a major goal.

As for his comments about 'weak guys? I already did some Fischer-Price percussion related to that subject, but I will add one more thought on that subject: The strongest people I know face up to their issues; the weakest I know run away from them—or deny them. The standard fight or flight orientation.

Not ever addressed is the fact that the mental game is intellectual, as well as psychological. Much of my work has little, if anything, to do with the "psyche." How to think, what to think and when to think—rationality—is about mental preparation, strategies and approaches to the game. And, oh yes, responses. Such as throwing equipment. Still unacceptable, after all these years.

Shortly after I started my full-time work with the Scott Boras Corporation, Scott and I were visiting his clients at a variety of spring training sites. Phoenix Municipal Stadium was one such site, the place where the A's play their exhibition games. At the end of a walkway behind the left field stands is an area where the media and people associated with the team gather after a game for the baseball fare of hotdogs, hamburgers and cold beverages and chatter.

As we walked toward the area, Scott said, "There's Billy Beane. I want to have a few words with him." I told him, in that case, I'd just turn around and wait for him at the exit. Scott would not have it. "Come with me. Aren't you guys tight?"

I told him we used to be, but since Billy's administrative advancements, we had lost contact. "Methinks he will flee when he turns to view my countenance." No, I didn't say that, but I did say I thought he'd go the other way when he spotted me. Scott did not immediately understand and insisted that I stay at his side.

As we entered the area, Scott turned to me. "That's funny (he *did* say that), Billy's disappeared." After a pause, "Is it because you know too much?"

I did not reply.

Billy's subsequent *Moneyball* protestations, read by me nearly seven years after public consumption, were initially agitating. Hours later, they became funny. When the opportunity arose for my acting career to be launched— appearance as a protagonist (antagonist?)—the whole deal became funnier still.

I did not have to curb my enthusiasm for my participation in the project. I had none. Now, if Betty Grable were alive and scripted to sidle up to me and sing, "Cuddle up a Little Closer," I would surely buckle.

Meanwhile, the reality is that I go on trying to do what many do not initially appreciate. On this topic, Al Leiter and Walt Weiss publicly put in their four cents some time ago: "It's clear many people don't want to hear the truth about themselves . . ." (Leiter), but "you get the truth from him, whether you like it or not."(Weiss) I guess Billy Beane did not like it. Funny, it took so long for him to express that feeling.

Shakespeare would know why.

Postscript: Well after my having completed this chapter, a baseball pal of mine contacted me and informed me that Oakland had hired a fellow to work in the area of sport psychology. "It's on a trial basis," said my source. The fellow was working exclusively with minor leaguers. (Maybe he can be in the movie, if he's still around when they begin to roll 'em.) I asked if Billy had acquiesced, because he knew almost every organization now employs someone to work in this capacity. "No," said my pal, "He's just throwing a bone. . . . You know Billy is anti-mental game/performance enhancement stuff." His actions betraying his ongoing protestations.

Curiouser and curiouser.

In late June, 2009, *Variety* ran a headline that announced: "Sony Scraps Soderbergh's 'Moneyball.'" The sub-heading: "Columbia Pictures drops ball on Brad Pitt pic."

Funnier and funnier.

Months later, another news release: A different company, a different producer, a different schedule. Same 'Funnyball.'

16

Fish Stories

One unpleasantness follows another. I might as well get this one onto the page now. Where to start? Well, my thoughts in the last chapter had to do with Oakland, and a related fish thought (the amazing capacity of the human brain to make obscure associations) immediately popped into my head. I was headed into the administrative office to see Sandy (not Billy Beane, who was still a scout then). As I passed through the waiting room and was just about to open the door to a hall leading to the offices, I heard a voice behind me.

"Young man!" (I was in my early 50's) Will you do me a favor?" The speaker was Joe DiMaggio. He had worked for the organization in past years, and, as every old baseball fan knows, he grew up in the Bay Area. "They are holding tickets for me back there for today's game, and I've been waiting for them for too long. Will you get them?"

"Only on one condition," I brashly said. He looked at me with considerable surprise. I was worried, lest he let loose with some blasphemy, so I quickly added, "On the condition you give me your autograph." He asked me if I had a piece of paper, and I told him I would get one right away. I went back into the corporate work place and asked a secretary for some paper (I always carry a pocket pen)—and for The Bronx Bomber's tickets. She asked me what the hell I was talking about. I identified Joe by the name she knew, took the paper and the tickets and returned to the waiting room.

I handed the icon his tickets first, then the paper and pen. He obliged without speaking. (He was an extremely reticent man, especially with strangers, so I did not ask him anything about Marilyn Monroe.)

I did say, "Hemingway was a big fan of yours." What was my problem? Awestruck, probably. Though I had rubbed elbows and psyches with some of the premium players of the day, I had not often been in the presence of those who performed on the large stage of my childhood. I had the same awkwardness when I'd spoken with Ted Williams at an Old-Timer's game in Fenway Park.

I had spoken about Ernest Hemingway in the office because my first thought, upon seeing Joltin' Joe sitting there, was the book, *The Old Man and the Sea.* In it, the old fisherman, Santiago, struggles desperately to land his 'big fish,' which fights him with determination. His admiration for the fish is comparable to what he feels for "the Great DiMaggio," and he articulates his respects for both marlin and Yankee.

But there I was in Oakland in the late '80's with my mind on a book I read in the mid-1950's. With my mind on that little boat off the coast of Cuba, remembering that I had not shared the great feeling of respect for Santiago's' adversary. Probably because, as a very young and sickly boy, in those early years, my life was ruled by two instincts: self-preservation and a hatred of fish. I had modified, somewhat, the first instinct.

Did I feel as I did because I had an unpleasant experience with a pet goldfish? No, it was because I had many unpleasant experiences with cod, trout, whitefish, herring, haddock, salmon, sole, and just for the halibut, carp. My mother was determined to have me eat fish. She was not skilled at deboning, and, on occasion, I would have been glad to choke to death if that could get me away from the table. (What an irony that would have been: an asthmatic who can't get his next breath because of a fish bone stuck in his throat.)

I had not been an enthusiastic carnivore either, but I soon became one. My fretful mother was happy to see me eat anything, so I stopped taking meat from my plate and stuffing it into the bottom of the trash basket under the sink (while she was out of the kitchen). Instead, I stuffed it into my mouth, simulating and practicing enjoyment as she bore witness to this phenomenon.

As I have said, as a bed-ridden child I was not exposed to outdoor activities. As a New York City adolescent (who was trying to make up for lost time) fishing was not *low* on my list—it was not *on* my list.

I have been informed that fishing is an ancient practice that dates back 40,000 years. Having an affinity for history and a love for my children, I determined that I would not project my negative bias of the practice on Melissa and Danny. "Why should my aversion for fish be passed on through the future generations of Dorfmans?" I asked myself. Besides, a fish on a hook was better than a fish on a plate. One that rested in front of *me*.

The subject of fishing had come into my mind when our family moved to Vermont. There in the town we lived was Orvis—fishing headquarters of . . . the world? One morning I entered its hallowed hall. I walked around the store, my eyes passing over fly rods and reels, fly lines, fly boxes, flies, vests, waders, books and whatnot-else. Manchester: a river ran through it. Arlington, actually. Close enough. Access to the Battenkill was minutes away, and by damn I was going to take my kids fishing. On it? At it? Certainly not *in* it, since I was never allowed to swim when I was a youngster, and had not taken the time to learn as an adult.

Pause: "A river ran through it." That reference, those words I am now came from a source of association back there in the recesses of my dark, damp unconscious. Perhaps it was fifteen years ago that I saw the film, "A River Runs Through It." So what was it that jumped out the dark and deep psychic river? Who, not what. It was Brad Pitt, the star of the river film—and possibly the celluloid Billy Beane. (My brain must be pickled like a herring, smoked liked a salmon. Muddled like a mullet? Enough Billy Beane.)

The over-solicitous Orvis salesman approached me. We exchanged greetings and I confessed that I was a neophyte and wanted to purchase only the basic necessities. They were provided for me—and for Melissa, age five, and Danny, three. On Saturday morning, the three of us drove five miles south to Arlington and west to a 'good spot' along the river. I parked at a safe spot off the road, and the three of us walked through high grass and weeds toward the river, rods held on our shoulders. I felt like Huck Finn.

I fished as if someone had slipped me a Mickey Finn. My first cast ("OK, watch me, kids"), caught in a branch of an over-hanging tree. The line stuck; my tugging exacerbated the problem. The kids had initially watched carefully, and, after a good look at my antics, mirthfully. In fact, they fell down laughing. I had to cut the line with my little Swiss knife-nail file-scissor, which I always carry in the pocket for such emergencies.

When hysteria (I had a form of it, as well, but its source was frustration, not mirth) subsided and a sense of decorum was re-established, I encouraged the kids to cast—carefully. They had already figured that out. The river was rapid but not deep where we had placed ourselves. I was watching Danny, who was upstream a bit, when I heard Melissa call: "Daddy, daddy. Help!" She was being carried down the river.

I ran in, ran after her. I couldn't have been swimming, after all. I splashed and thrashed, until I had her in my grasp. I pulled her out. As is the general case with children, they are fine as soon as crisis is over. As is the case with adult parents, they are fine during the crisis and not-so-fine after it.

The highlight of the experience, insofar as there was a highlight, was, for the children, my removing my wallet from the pocket of dripping pants and placing bills of various dollar denominations on the rock, so they could dry in the sun as the children continued their activity—such as it was.

No fish were caught that day. No fish were caught any day, because, on my list of future family pursuits, all other possibilities ascended. Is it more appropriate to say that fishing plummeted? Disappeared?

Being an admirer of the ancient Greeks and their philosophy, I was happy to read, some years after the Battenkill fiasco, that fishing had a very low status in Greek culture. How fine that I had unknowingly adopted a precept of Socratic wisdom, which I much admired and strove for always.

On a crowded shelf, my eye was drawn to a book title: *The Compleat Angler*. I took it into my hands with the same feeling I have when I push my tongue into an aching tooth. As I flipped the pages, the ache very apparent, I saw poems and songs about fishing. Folklore, stories—and, oh, for chrissake, *recipes*! I slammed the book shut and left the otherwise beloved Mark Skinner library.

Life was pleasant and busy in Vermont. But in 1974, Anita and I decided to broaden our vista and visit her parents' homeland during our summer break from teaching. We took the children, who were then ten and eight years old. Off we flew into a yonder that would ultimately be above Åland. Helsinki, actually, where we would board a ferry taking us to our final destination.

The Åland Islands form an archipelago in the Baltic. Anita's family lived on the main island, along with ninety percent of the population. To the east of the mainland, in the Baltic Sea—between Sweden and Finland—are approximately 6,500 tiny islands and skerries.

Anita had at least fifty first cousins there at the time, and one of her favorites had already visited us in Vermont with his wife and young boys. (One of them, as I wrote in an earlier volume, would live with us for an academic year, attending the high school at which I taught.) Anita's favorite cousin, Leif, had two brothers, Ålanke and Henry. Each had a distinct personality, but all three were engaging and happy, as were their wives, to be our hosts and hostesses. Fishing, need I say, was a regular recreational activity on the island, a source of food—and a viable industry.

Shortly after our arrival, the cousins rounded up the children for some sport. We climbed into a couple of boats and motored out into the sea. We each were placed on a skerry—a rock more than large enough for an individual or a small group to occupy. Their sizes varied, but they were all far enough apart for someone to climb onto his own rock and watch a cousin speed away to drop off other individuals, young and old, like mail bags.

The rod and reel provided for me rested at my feet as I adjusted my baseball hat, stalling for time until the boat was far enough away. Then I picked up my equipment, stared at it, fumbled with it—and decided I had to cast sooner or later. Sooner. I was among experts. So what? Form be damned; I hurled my line into the Baltic Sea.

The hook somehow became caught on something. I pulled. I pulled again. Did I have a big one on my first cast? I did indeed: a big skerry. The hook was stuck under my rock. How the hell did that happen? Before I could answer (I could never have answered, of course), a cousin came speeding back to my fishing ground. "How did he get here so fast?" I asked myself. The answer should have been obvious. He had been watching and waiting. How did he know? I'll never know.

His smile had in it the co-mingling of the familial affection for a challenged child and a superior sarcasm for a bungling American who happened to marry a beloved cousin. He freed the hook and sped off without a word. I tentatively dropped my line into the sea and waited for Godot.

On the way back to shore, I said with magnanimous self-effacement to Leif's oldest son, Jens, "That's pretty hard to do, not catch a fish in the middle of the Baltic Ocean."

He called me and raised me: "That's hard to do, catch your line under a rock in the Baltic Sea."

I was happy to reach land again, after that trying excursion.

All was forgiven, if not forgotten. We had a good time that night, and I was invited to join a group of four to go back into the Baltic the next day. My first response was tentative. They probably knew it would be, so one of them explained quickly, "We put nets out every day. In the morning we go out and empty them."

Hell, I can empty a net—can't I? So I nodded with feigned enthusiasm. Early morning, he might have mentioned. At 5:30 am five of us were in the boat. We sped out beyond the scene of yesterday's outing, farther into the Baltic. After fifteen minutes had passed, we arrived at a marker. The cousins got right to it, reaching and hauling and twisting a large net into the boat. Then dumping and pulling small fish into large pails. I 'helped' with the twisting. Enough about my contribution.

After a time, the nets were properly placed back into the sea, and off we sped. Another cousin waited for our arrival. He had started a fire and prepared a small area. Breakfast was to be served. Fish, the main course. "This can't be happening," I thought.

Anticipation is worse than participation. That's a line I very often use in my work. It's true when I say it, and it was true years before I ever said it. What actually happened was that the damn fish tasted—delicious. Strömming, they are called: small Baltic herrings. They were fried over a hot flame as we sat near the shore drinking beer, instead of orange juice. By the time the small things were set before me, the beer-before-daybreak had made anything acceptable to my senses, taste included.

But as I suggested, the strömming were "extraordinary," a word chosen in an alcoholic state for the cousins' sake. (As if I knew what 'ordinary' strömming tasted like). Adding to the wonder of the breakfast were wonderful small potatoes that accompanied the—fish. Bread was torn from loaves, and as we ate and drank, I felt like Zorba the Swede. The morning more than compensated for the previous day.

Many memories still come from that trip; many stories. It was a particularly wonderful experience for Melissa and Danny.

Now, years after my employment as a Marlin and a Devil Ray (one of life's many jokes), Anita and I sit on the deck of our North Carolina house on sunny afternoons and look out over a small lake. It is man-made, but it is scenic—and stocked with fish. I need not say that my activity and appreciation are confined to viewing. Dan and his son, Riley, have been coming over since we moved a mile down the mountain six years ago to this house. They both enjoy fishing on the lake.

Riley's first rod-and-reel experience was as a five or six-year old. He was quite excited as he came through our front door, went out of the house through the kitchen door, sped down the steps of the deck and walked briskly toward the dock. He turned as he walked and shouted to me, "Grandpa, come and watch."

Watch?

His father must have forewarned him.

17

The Weather Within

My father stopped me as I was headed out of our apartment. I was a high-schooler at the time. "Are you feeling better today?" he asked. I had been breathing pretty well and feeling—physically—as well as I ever had.

"Fine," I said, with confusion written on my face.

"Oh, then your rectumitis is improving?"

I asked him what he was talking about. "What's rectumitis?"

"It's an inflammation of the nerve that runs from your asshole to your eyeball and gives you a shitty outlook on life. I presumed you were suffering from it."

I did not respond, so he elaborated. "Your attitude has been observably poor lately. What's going on?"

I still did not respond, because I didn't know what was "going on." I had not been troubled by a particular crisis or an unpleasant anticipation. I stood in the narrow hallway which led to the door. He turned and went into the kitchen.

My mother had heard the exchange. She said to my father, "Oh, he probably got out on the wrong side of the bed." My father, a quick wit as well as a keen observer, said, "That explains it; he's been banging his head for a week. That has to affect a person." (One side of my bed butted up against a wall.)

That was not at all what he was thinking about, I felt. He was talking about an attitude that encompassed beliefs—and choices. Was I feeling guilty? Whatever else I felt, I felt like getting out of there, and I made a hasty exit.

I cannot say how many times I have heard that "wrong side of the bed" business over the course of my life—since then. Most often, however, it is an explanation provided by someone who has been asked about his prevailing attitude—or mood. It is not, as award-winning actress Marissa Tomei said on the witness stand in ("My Cousin Vinnie"), "a bullshit question." It is a bullshit *answer*.

When speaking about 'attitude,' I make a semantic distinction. An attitude is not the same as a mood. Good attitude; good mood. Bad attitude; bad mood. Not the same. In my vernacular, 'attitude' refers to an *on-going* state of mind a person has as he approaches or experiences his life. Mood is a *temporary* state. That is the way I consider and define the terms. When my father told me I had a bad attitude, he was trying to say I had, in the recent historical past, an on-going lousy mood, which became a bad attitude by dint of longevity. Much ado about nothing? Well, it is *something* I wish to make clear.

Something else I wish to clarify. I am not interested in speaking here about *social* attitudes; pro-life or pro-choice, policies on immigration and such. My interest is in the more *personal* attitudes. Those that are held and made evident and on display daily. Nor do I speak about a disposition such as Hamlet's, an emotional, affective disorder or depression that leads him to thoughts of suicide. The more basic, good-old-fashioned 'lousy mood syndrome' doesn't apply here either.

In baseball clubhouses (and everywhere else, for that matter), I have come across many guys who were in awful moods, myself included. Significantly fewer have been counted among those I considered to have bad attitudes. Though I've had times when my moods were dark, and I withdrew deep into my internal cave, I did not suddenly run there. It has never (?) been a 'mood swing.' Rather, it's been a gradual effect (I most often do not know the cause), something akin to a time-release pill. These moods (exactly like those of one of my older sisters, though mine have been less frequent) I wore proudly as a young man, believing myself to be a Lincoln-like sufferer of melancholia. (I still believe that, sort of.)

But my *attitude* is quite something else. It is built by thoughts, whereas my mood is built by emotions (feelings).

I understand and accept (and relish) the fact that I have the capacity to control the manner in which I assess my world and respond to it. Each year, each day, each moment. My attitude influences most everything I do, and my daily goal is to assert control over it, rather than forfeiting if allowing whatever external influences arise to have dominion over the way I think and act.

When I have not been in control, for whatever the reason may have been, I have been hurtful, spiteful, vengeful and just plain nasty. As unpleasant as these infrequent occurrences have been, they have allowed me to step back and recognize what can happen when someone loses control of the self he believes himself to be. A someone he aspires to be. Such circumstances provoked behaviors I did not consider to be representative of my actual attitudinal corpus. I acted in a manner contrary to my true self, and betrayed that self as I did so.

Though my prevailing attitude (philosophy of life?) was unchanged when these lesser angels (devils!) took over my inner dwelling place, I had nevertheless opened the door for them. They were happy to enter and do their damage. Yet, they were unwelcome—and my relief was palpable when they left. Did I act aggressively and push them out? (Regaining control.) Or did I sit inert, waiting until they decided to leave? (Submissive non-resistance.) I always sought answers for these questions, for future reference.

I bother to speak about all this because my attitude indirectly defines me. My *actions* do so *directly*, and they determine the way I interpret and respond to all the matters and issues and people and tasks I face on a daily basis.

So let me (finally) get to the point. People can *change* their attitudes. A couple of chapters ago I wrote about a man who denied this ability, for his own purposes and, I believe, to his detriment. Awareness is a first step. People must recognize what attitudes they hold and reveal to others. Unfortunately, introspection is not a regular, daily activity of mass man. And being honest about oneself is not in many people's playbook. I speak from the experiences I have had during my fifty-three years as an educator and counselor.

Many people I have confronted about their less-than-desirable attitudes have responded to me by saying exactly what one major league manager said: (I wrote about him in an earlier volume.): "That's just the way I am." He was fired, not because he couldn't change, but because he wouldn't. He, of course, took the stance of pre-determination.

A little digression here. I was listening to a Linda Eder CD the other night. She sang a song from *La Cage Aux Folles* entitled "I Am What I Am." I thought sounded like the manager I'm going to write about. "That's just the way I am" was his battle cry also, right? Wrong. Linda Eder was not singing about a battle to defend—to rationalize—a reluctance to change an attitude she was destined to have. She sang in declaration of an attitude she had formed—and, take it or leave it, fella and madam—that is who I am. Defiance can be clothed in a variety of outfits.

Where was I? Oh, yes, that manager again. He explained himself in the same manner as others who prefer the personal *status quo*. It is easier for them to say their attitude has been pre-determined than say they're stubborn asses.

A person tells me he's aware of his 'bad attitude.' He has evaluated himself honestly and is ready to make a change. What next? As football analyst Lee Corso would say, not so fast, my friend. An important aid to a self-awareness of effect is the revelation of the cause of the attitude. Has it been passed on by a parent? (By example or indoctrination, not genes.) Is the manner in which the individual was brought up the cause? Or is it other environmental factors? Teachers? Peers? Those discoveries are not to be used as excuses, but as reasons. (A distinction not made by the hard-ass—and stupid—mentality that sticks to the belief that an attribution is the same as an excuse.)

A number of players I have dealt with were abused when they were children. Once we had gotten through all the identification, history and understanding—causal factors—I said this to them: "Now we know why you are what you are, why your attitude is what it is. Fine, that's the end of that. From now on, all we care about is *who you want to be, what attitudes you want to possess*—and *how we can accomplish* that. (Strategies.)

So, first a person is aware of his views and behaviors, then he discovers why he believes and acts as he does—and then ---- he must identify the characteristics of a good attitude, or the attitude he wishes to possess. For example, he wants to be open-minded, rather than closed minded; he'd rather be enthusiastic about his daily activities, rather than starting the day saying to himself (or others, since my ears have been on the receiving end), "Different day, same shit."). He might want to have an interest in others, rather than immersing himself in his own "shit." Does he want to shut his mouth (especially since what came out of it was incrementally excremental) and listen to other people's points of view? Be an optimist, rather than a pessimist? Committed rather than indifferent? Co-operative vs. uncooperative? Responsible vs. irresponsible? And so on.

Many of us are capable of figuring out what is better for our mental state. Our mental health. Many others need some assistance. Still others, even after self-examination, find they are (rightfully) pleased by their attitudes. Whether it be in calm or troubled waters, the relationship between the sailor's attitude and his voyage should be clear. A troubled sailor usually has a troubling voyage.

Viktor Frankl, in the profound book I referred to in a previous chapter, speaks of our ability to be self-determining. "Man does not simply exist," Frankl writes, "but always decides what his existence will be. . . (E)very human being has the freedom to change at any instant. . . . The last of the human freedoms is to choose one's attitude in any given set of circumstances, to choose one's own way."

In other words, we aren't bound to be tomorrow what we have been today; we are not bound to act tomorrow as we have acted today. We have the freedom to make a choice about our attitude.

Athletes I've come across who were considered to have bad attitudes are, as their teammates so directly put it, 'clueless' about all this. The ones with good attitudes act like 'free' people, and they are healthier and happier—and greatly valued by their teammates and coaches. And they play to their peak far more consistently than 'bad apples.' They *always* contribute to the team—by their example alone.

The major benefit, in my view, is that they are free. Athletes—people— with poor attitudes are unhappy. They are victims of their own weakness, quick to blame circumstance or other people when confronted about unacceptable behavior. They have forfeited their freedom. They wait for the world to make them happy. It does not happen often, and when it does, it doesn't last very long.

Almost all of the athletes I've had a working relationship with have come to understand the difference between a good attitude and a bad one. I would further say that almost all appreciated the benefits of having a healthy attitude. And so did the people with whom they came in contact. Oscar Wilde shed brilliant light on people with good attitudes and those with bad ones. In his own wry manner he noted how the possessors of the opposing attitudes can, in their unique way, please the people who meet them. "Some cause happiness wherever they go; others, whenever they go."

Yes, I have often thought, when a bad-attitude guy entered my room, "Don't let the door hit you in the ass on the way out." Habit is stronger than reason. Some people I have tried to assist were too comfortable in their habits. Others just did not have the personal strength and self-discipline to sustain their efforts to change. They remained victims of the bad habits their attitudes created, retaining what Chesterton called "a bad smell in the mind." My disinfectant wasn't strong enough, I admit.

My greatest efforts continue to be devoted to the self I, myself, bring to each day. Climate control, I call it. I am my own meteorologist. But I do not forecast and describe. I am one who controls and *creates* the weather. The weather of my inner world. And while Anita does her annual spring cleaning in and around the house, I follow the advice (not *all* of it, to tell the truth) offered by one of the characters in Peter Weiss's play, *Marat/Sade*: "The important thing is to pull yourself up by your own hair to turn yourself inside out and see the whole world with fresh eyes."

The hair part? Well, with my new hips in place, I just rise easily out of my chair. I have a protective attitude toward the hair that remains on my head.

18

A Special Kid

When I first began my work in baseball, I was a few months south of fifty-years in age. I had taught for twenty-seven years, and I transferred my habitual referent—'kid'—from students to players. In 1997, I apologized to veteran catcher Darren Daulton for calling him 'kid.' (He was thirty-five at the time.) He responded, "Harv, you can call *anyone* in this clubhouse 'kid'." (I was sixty-two at the time.)

And I continued to do just that. Each day, for example, I would greet Andre Dawson, then forty-three years old, with a smile and, "How'ya doing, kid." (After a wait that took him out of 'Kidhood,' Andre was finally voted into the Baseball Hall of Fame this year, 2010.)

He would return the smile, accompanied by "Good, doc."

The "kid" I refer to in the chapter's title was born in 1979. July 19th to be exact. We first faced each other in front of a hotel elevator door in West Palm Beach, Florida. A day in March, 2000. Richard Ankiel, Jr.—Rick, to many, "Ank" to most—was at spring training with the St. Louis Cardinals. He was a Boras client, given 2.5 million dollars for signing out of high school as a pitching phenom at Port St. Lucie High School in Florida. *USA Today* named him High School Player of the Year in 1997.

His brief minor league career was equally impressive: Texas League All-Star pitcher, Double-A All-Star starting pitcher, Cardinals Minor League Player of the Year and *Baseball America* first-team Minor League All-Star starting pitcher.

Standing in front of the elevator in West Palm was one of the most outstanding pitching prospects to come along in years. And that was not *me*.

"Hey, Rick," I said—and introduced myself as a Scott Boras guy. I did mention sport psychology. I do not think he heard the "sport" part. This was a very high-profile 'kid'—in every sensible sense of the word. Scott wanted me to get in front of him and cultivate a relationship. I had been told that Ankiel's chronological and maturational ages were disparate. My visit did not have a casual, social intention. This was serious business.

"Do you have a few minutes this evening?" I asked. He seemed to be counting the seconds until the elevator arrived.

"I can't," he said. "I have a dinner appointment with my family."

Maybe. Maybe not, I thought. "That's fine," I said with great understanding. "But I'm staying at this hotel tonight, and I want you at my room at 8:30 tomorrow morning." He seemed stunned by the declaration and the dictatorial style. He had time to nod his head before the elevator doors closed on him.

The knock on the door came at 8:25, a good start. As he swept past me into the room, he said, "You want me to lay down on the couch?" His anticipatory dread was shabbily clothed in humor.

"Sitting up will be fine," I said. I spent the next thirty-five minutes talking about the mental approach to pitching. I said nothing remotely connected to his family or personal life, much of which was troubling to me and, certainly, troublesome to him. His great relief was evident at the end of our one-hour meeting. We had got it off.

As he was leaving, he turned to me and said, "Do you play golf?" (Almost as bad as asking if I fished. I came to know him as a lover of that 'sport'—a fishing aficionado in the early developmental stage.) I told him I did not, but we would have a good fish dinner together soon. Another nod—and he was gone.

That was how our relationship began.

How has it continued? With greater and greater depth. With greater and greater trust; with greater and greater mutual caring. So much has been written about Rick Ankiel that I am reluctant to hear myself 'talk' about his history—on and off the field. But having chosen to write this chapter (we had on one desperate occasion discussed a book). I must provide some details.

His high school senior year is the logical place to start, because his 11-1 record (with an earned run average of 0.47) drew the attention of major league scouts. (As did his 162 strikeouts in 74 innings pitched.)

As noted, he was later named Minor League Player of the Universe or some such designation during his stay there—which was not a long one. His first major league game was in Montreal near the end of the 1999 season. The following season was his first full year at the big league level. At the age of twenty, (he was the second youngest player in the league), he won 11 and lost 7. His earned run average (3.50) was ninth in the National League. He struck out 194 batters—at a rate of 9.98 strikeouts per nine innings (second in the league to Randy Johnson). He was second in the Rookie of the Year voting (to Rafael Furcal of the Braves).

Ank's fastball was clocked at 94-97 miles an hour. He threw a sinker that had great movement and some compared his curveball to the one thrown by Sandy Koufax. A flamboyant, blithe spirit, Ank had the world, in baseball vernacular, by the short and curlies. Until the end of that fateful summer.

So much has been written about the disaster—and he and I have discussed it *ad nauseum* (to both of us) that I will put it as succinctly as possible. The Cardinals won their division in 2000. Assessments that include finger-pointing, rationalization, wrong-headedness and plain ignorance can still be heard when the question comes up, as it still does eleven years later. That question is: should a twenty-one-year-old rookie be the starting pitcher for the first game of the post season? As I said, I will not go deeply into all that. Anyone can Google himself to ecstasy tracking down all the prevailing views.

My own, for what it's worth, is he should *not* have been the starting pitcher. Is that brilliance in retrospect? Well, it's not brilliance in any aspect. But at the time, I was unhappy about Tony LaRussa's decision. I had been there before (in Oakland) and seen young pitchers rushed into situations beyond their emotional capabilities to cope. Tony and I had a 3am phone 'discussion' about such a situation. I lost that argument years before Ank's fateful fall and, to my mind, the young Oakland pitcher lost his career. So did Ank.

The rest, which is indeed history, does not offer a pretty picture. Ank worked himself out of difficulty in the first two innings before imploding in the third inning, when he gave up two hits, walked four batters, threw five wild pitches, and was removed from the game. I still see that picture—those wild pitches. So does Ank. I remember how I felt as I watched. Ank still remembers how he felt as he fought to survive.

But at the time—after the game—in typical fashion, he laughed it off, repeating the tidbit so helpfully provided by a media moron: "I'm the first guy to throw five wild pitches in an inning since some guy did it in 1890."

His later appearances in the series were more of the same. The Dreaded Thing was on the scene. As it was the following season, when he walked twenty-five batters in twenty-four innings—and threw five wild pitches. He was sent to the Triple A team, where matters got worse. We had spoken, but Ank was not allowing his true feelings to express themselves. This was nothing unusual for him, but I told him if he wanted to attack this problem, a rather intense and intrusive (my interpretation of how he would view it) intervention was required.

I will not go into details of that intervention, but I will say that our relationship, founded on eventual mutual trust, was an extraordinary experience for me. What he had to come to terms with was enormous. It included dealing with a father who, as one journalist put it, "failed (his son) when he needed him most." I would say a child in his formative years needs his father "most," but the senior Ankiel had been an instrument for destruction since Ank went on the playing field as a youngster. Now the father was in jail, serving six years for dealing in drugs and calling on his son to pay lawyers' fees and provide money for whatever other legitimate or illegitimate needs he had. Ank's older brother was also serving time for the same offense. The mother eventually divorced her husband. She had issues of her own. Enough said about family 'support.'

Ank's thought and feelings were as disoriented as his pitches. He was flying upside down trying to find the control panel. Where could his mind go for respite? Given his family history, that worried me.

Some good fortune came in the midst of all this. Ank was sent all the way down to the Cardinals' rookie league team in Johnson City, Tennessee. It was an hour drive from my home in North Carolina, so I could visit with him regularly. He had already confronted many difficult personal tasks, including the writing of a letter to his father declaring independence—personal and financial. His self-esteem, never developed, owing to constant negative signals sent his way from early years on, was now, Ank believed, ready to be addressed—planted, so to speak. He learned techniques for cultivating, fertilizing and watering. A sprout appeared—and slowly grew.

Ank laughed after the fact. The facts at Johnson City: Rookie Level Player of the Year, Appalachian League All-Star left-handed pitcher, Rookie League All-Star starting pitcher, Appalachian League Pitcher of the Year, and Appalachian League All-Star designated hitter. (He had a .638 slugging percentage, ten homeruns and 35 RBI in 105 at-bats, a portend of things to come.)

"I was second in the *big* leagues as Rookie of the Year, so I really can't take all this seriously." But he did, down deep—where it mattered. It was, to my mind, a greater achievement than what he had done as a big league rookie, and I told him so—and why.

The following season was no laughing matter. He missed all of 2002 with an elbow problem. When he was cleared to pitch again—in 2003—he was again ineffective: wild and without a sense of purpose. Trying to compete effectively and protect his arm at the same time, he accomplished neither. In July, he required Tommy John surgery.

Much time was spent on the phone with Cardinals GM, Walt Jocketty, an old Oakland pal of mine. Walt asked me to speak with Tony and Dave Duncan (pitching coach) on how to best deal with Ank, his program, the media and whatever else needed to be done to best achieve some sane approach to Ank's return to big-league spring training in 2004. Tony and Dunc were open and cooperative—and concerned. They certainly liked the kid, as did anyone who came in contact with him. He had worked (too hard) at pleasing all his previous life. ("This," I told him, "is going to change." No more Mister Nice-Guy?)

Ank's return to the big leagues was an anxious moment—for both of us. I felt the way I did watching Melissa at her first ballet recital as a child. And Danny at his first (and last, he was happy to know) Little League tryout. The size and scope of the situation is irrelevant. It is the size of the care the spectator has for the performer that is affecting—and I was affected. (As Anita had told me, "I have never seen you become so emotionally involved with a player the way you are with Ank." She was right. The fact of the matter is I didn't feel for the kid; I felt *with* him)

Ank rose to the occasion. Here I must say that the most difficult task one can have is facing the environment in which one has been traumatized. Traumatic memory, I have already written in a previous chapter ("The Dreaded Thing") is always there. It must be confronted if it is to be, at least, diminished in size and strength. Ank confronted it on the same mound in St. Louis that had been the launching pad for all those errant pitches. The St. Louis fans gave him a standing ovation when he entered the game as a relief pitcher. He struck out five of the first six batters he faced. He received another ovation when he departed.

In the minor leagues that season he had walked only two batters in twenty-three and two-thirds innings. He struck out twenty-three. In the big leagues that season he walked one batter and struck out nine in ten innings of work. Had he cured the disease? It is never cured, I hold, it is only in remission.

Remission remained in Puerto Rico that winter, where Ank continued to pitch effectively. But in spring training, 2005, Ank called. "I just had a shitty bullpen (session)." I told him he had a couple of them before, but responded well the next time. He said to me what I had heard before from pitcher John Burke.

(This already noted in Chapter 11: John told me, "I get up very day and have to face the demons. I know I can beat them—have beaten them—but the fight is exhausting. Playing just isn't fun." Rick's message was essentially the same. "The energy it takes; the anticipation of going to the field with the strength you need isn't the same as going there with joy. It's just got to a point where it's wearing me down mentally.")

During that phone conversation, Ank told me he thought he might be able to become an outfielder. Just like that. Walt Jocketty had been open to the idea—perhaps even had initiated it, I don't remember. I do remember Ank and I talking about all the possibilities that might be considered, should his playing career be over. (It was in Johnson City that we mulled over—and abandoned—the idea of our doing a book. Eventually, there will be one about Rick Ankiel, I am certain, but I will not write it.)

He was extremely popular with the hometown fans, the coaching staff and teammates. They encouraged him to continue in baseball—and so his wish to be an outfielder became a reality. Off he went to the Cardinals' Class A minor league team at the beginning of 2005. His slugging percentage there was .514. He was promoted to Double A, where he slugged .515. Could this be possible?

The Cardinals were determined to find out. They invited him—as an outfielder, of course—to major league spring training camp in 2006. His defense was impressive, his arm strong. His left knee, alas, was injured during a spring training game. In May, Ank had season-ending surgery.

But he showed up at spring training the following season, 2007. LaRussa, almost apologetically (guilt again?) said that Ank would be better off playing at the Triple A level than sitting on the Cardinals bench. "It isn't because he isn't capable," LaRussa explained. "But unless you can guarantee that he would get 400 or 500 at-bats, it would be a bad move for him and for us." The fact that so much deference was being given to someone who hadn't been a position player at the big league level is disconcerting, to say the least. Remarkable, to say the most.

On Memorial Day, playing in Round Rock, Texas, Ank had a big game: two home runs and an over-the-shoulder catch that prevented two runs from scoring. Two months later, he was selected as a starting outfielder for the Triple-A All-Star team.

By August 8, his numbers were impressive enough to get the attention of the Cardinals brass: 32 homers, 89 RBI, a .267 batting average. On August 9, he was called up to the big club. He had been leading the Pacific Coast League in home runs and was second in RBI.

His return was triumphant. Batting second and playing right field, Ankiel was given a prolonged standing ovation by the St. Louis fans. In his fourth at-bat of the game, he hit a three-run homer. The Cardinals won the game, 5-0. He became the first pitcher since Clint Hartung (1947 Giants) to hit his first major league home run as a pitcher and, later, hit one as a position player. Babe Ruth preceded Hartung in that achievement.

Two days later, Ank received three standing O's. He went 3-4 batting, including two homers, and made an outstanding, run-saving catch in right field. Naturally, the media was all over the event. A syndicated columnist by the name of Charles Krauthammer wrote, "His return after seven years—if only three days long—is the stuff of legends. . . . The Natural returns to St. Louis." Inspiring, if hyperbolic.

On the last day of the month, Ank hit his first grand slam home run—off a formidable left-handed reliever named Eddie Guardado. Despite what I considered to be too many strikeouts (many others shared the thought), Ank finished the 2007 season with a batting average of .285. In two months he had hit 11 homers and 39 RBI, with a slugging percentage of .535.

The bloom came off the rose when Ank admitted to using HGH, after having had Tommy John surgery on his elbow. HGH was not banned by Major League Baseball until 2005, well after Ank's use of the medication, which was prescribed for him by a doctor. I remember the phone conversation and Ank's concern—and his reporting of the doctor's assurances that it would have a medical benefit by stimulating "synthesis of collagen"—whatever-the-hell that is—and help expedite the recovery process after the surgery.

Major League Baseball concluded there was no evidence of wrong-doing, but Ank was upset because he was being thrown in the pile with violators and suspected violators. "I took these meds while I was still a pitcher, for shit's sake," he said to me, venting. I knew full well.

"This too shall pass," I told him. And it did.

In 2008, Ank batted .264, had 25 home runs and 71 runs batted in. He became the second player in major league history to hit twenty-five homers in a season and win 25 or more games as a pitcher. The other: Babe Ruth. A guy named Reb Russell won 74 games as a pitcher for the White Sox between 1913 and 1919 and hit 21 homers as an outfielder during two years with the Pirates (1919 – 1920). Anyhow, a pretty fine accomplishment.

Two throws—both in the same game—drew great attention to his arm again. "The first one was impressive," said teammate Troy Glaus, who took the throw on a line from deep center field and tagged an astonished runner out at third. "The second one was shocking, I would say," Glaus said. "I think everybody was kind of in awe. How do you put into words something you've never seen?"

What he had never seen was a throw made on a line from the deepest reaches of center field, Ank's back just about against the wall, and that hit the spot on the third-base bag where Glaus' glove just took it and applied the tag to an *astounded* base runner.

Ank told the media, "It felt good. I hit a homer that day, too, and it just doesn't even compare. I mean anybody can hit a homer." Right.

LaRussa was asked which throw he thought was better. "It's like grading A+ and A++," he said. "It just totally lit up the dugout." To me, there was no doubt that the second throw—from a significantly further distance—was the more spectacular. Glaus agreed. "Not only the pure velocity," Glaus said in wonder, "It was dead on the line. A foot and a half either way and we're not having this conversation," he told a reporter. Dead on line from 300 feet-plus. "And in the air the whole way," Glaus said, almost talking to himself. Thinking about Ank's troubles when he was a pitcher, Glaus said, with a sense of irony, "Maybe sixty feet was too close."

Many a truth is said in jest. No player with throwing problems that I've ever dealt with—or heard about—was an outfielder. In fact (Dale Murphy another fine example) playing outfield abetted the problem. The first thing I have pitchers do—some who can't even play catch from thirty feet—is called long toss. The player extends his arm—and 'airs out' the throw. No problem. But this is a digression.

The 2009 season was a disappointment. It began well enough, but a couple of months in Ank made a spectacular catch in left center field. He was greeted by appreciative fan applause and an unforgiving wall. He jammed his neck and shoulder, was put on the disabled list—and, I believe, returned too soon. His body was not ready and his mental approach suffered as a result. Not the first guy to do that; not the last.

"I made the catch," he told me proudly. I had seen it on Direct TV. He was carted off the field and diagnosed with "whiplash." His entire body pained him, he said. Chest, back, head. He insisted on trying to play through it. We discussed the issue at length. Eventually, he was put on the Disabled List. It should have been done sooner.

When he returned, he was not fit. This I knew because we spoke every day and discussed—among many other topics—his physical state. As LaRussa had described Ank to the media, "He's very competitive." Mildly put.

"The Natural" was more or less a story of the past. The life span of media attention is in accordance with extremes: spectacular success and colossal failure. Ank had received both. Now, because his performance went from mediocre to dismal, by the time the All-Star break arrived, he was not under the radar; he was off it. A case of the good news—and the bad. The bad being a batting average below .220, with five homers and twenty-two runs batted in. He struggled mightily.

The trainer had implored him to have an MRI, feeling that the shoulder he jammed into the fence was "not right." Ank explained to me that he had already missed over two full years with injuries. "Now (months before) I went on the DL again—and what happens if the MRI shows something?"

"What happens," I said, "is that it would explain all the difficulties you've been having driving the ball—and it would keep you off the field, where you don't belong if you're not fit to compete at the level you should." Ank is intelligent. As with many of the players who respond to my remarks with, "I know," Ank knew. And as is the case with other players, he just needs to hear it and be prodded to do what he knows. (Oakland pitcher Bob Welch referred to me somewhat endearingly as "Jiminy Fucking Cricket." The conscience that was his guide.)

Ank struggled mightily at the end of the season, 'losing his swing,' his confidence, and the trust the manager had in him. He was used sparingly: two post-season appearances as a pinch hitter. He struck out both times. And now, as I write this, Rick Ankiel is a free agent. It is my view, his view and the view of onlookers that he will not return to the Cardinals. I think he needs a fresh atmosphere—and the benefits that come with the freshness and a freedom from presumed familiarity. From limited definition. From all the complicated impulses of a manager who was trying to right a wrong. From a self-consciousness that limits the ability to grow out of the box built by others—the well-meaning and the casually judgmental.

I just went into the back room, where the photocopier and filing cabinets—and personal pictures with inscriptions hang with privacy. I will share the words Ank wrote a good number of years ago, when he was first becoming my 'special kid.' We had gone pretty deep into his being. He was seeing and understanding plenty that had not been apparent (or of 'interest') to him previously. The concluding words he wrote on the picture are, ". . . and helping me start to become the person I want to become." The process should be on-going—for all of us.

I was very disappointed that Anita and I could not attend Ank's wedding. He understood. "Yeah, I know that doctor of yours is treating you like Bubble Boy." Ank married Lory Bailey after the midnight on New Year's Eve. So, technically, they were wed on January 1, 2007. I had previously dined with Ank and Lory, so I knew her well enough to be happy for him—and for her. They visited us in North Carolina after the 2007 season. He 'dropped in' en route to spring training, 2010.

Ank's father is out of jail and out of his son's life. In just noting that, I get a feeling of discomfort. Actually, this entire chapter is discomforting. Here's why. Upon reading what I've written, I am fully aware that most of it is impersonal and based on his athletic achievements and difficulties. Plenty of statistics. Boring. But our relationship is a very personal one and, invoking professional 'confidentiality' makes it easy for me to avoid saying anything that might be interesting and insightful. Unfortunate. That is the approach I decided upon.

The need I had for this chapter's inclusion is based on the significance this relationship has in my life. So, am I saying, "This means a lot to me, but I can't share it with you"? That probably sums it up. I have shared many personal aspects of my life, but it is not appropriate, I think, to share insights that began on a professional level and ended up being very personal. Insights about someone *else*. So be it.

The following comes from the reports I received on October 11, 2009: "St. Louis Cardinals outfielder Rick Ankiel slipped out the back door of Busch Stadium late Sunday morning, perhaps for the final time. After telling reporters he wanted to finish packing before taking questions about the season and his future, Ankiel rolled the final load to his car and drove away."

He drove to his fall destination, home in Jupiter, Florida. After his February, 2010, visit, Ank headed to Arizona, where he would train with his new team, the Kansas City Royals.

Have I mentioned that I love this kid?

19

Books, Books, Books

"... (T)he person I want to become," Rick Ankiel had written on his photo. When I first read those words, I asked myself, "At the age he inscribed that thought, Ank was twenty-three. What did *I* want to become at that age?" I had no clue. I seem to recall that I was becoming without 'wanting' to become. I was a mindless camel humping along aimlessly on the vast desert of life, having departed from the oasis called 'college.'

I knew what I did not want to become—or remain. Vulnerable, weak, socially uncertain and malleable. Hardly life-goals, but understandably important, given the nature of my early years.

Ortega Y Gasset, the Spanish philosopher and professor, wrote, "Tell me to what you pay attention and I will tell you who you are." He was a smart guy, but I think he over-estimated his abilities as an analyst. Still, when thinking about myself—and, in this case, writing about myself, I must give him great credit for the assessment, incomplete as it may be. Just as we are more complicated than our thoughts, we are more entire than our interests. Still . . .

Gasset's line was not his most well-known pronouncement. His more famous maxim also related to identity: *"Yo soy y mi cimrcumstancia"*—I am myself and my circumstances.

Essentially, he was saying that we are a combination of our being and our immediate personal world—and that the things that we are most attentive to—interested in—define us. His words lead one to believe the definition is complete. I believe it is incomplete.

Nevertheless, I continue to think back on those matters to which I *have* given a great percentage of my time and most of my attention. Books are right up there. In fact, if work is eliminated from consideration, books become Number One. This all started, as I wrote in the first volume of this trilogy, in a bed, where breathing—actually the attempt—was the major activity of the day. The radio came second, tallying the types of cars that passed on the streets below my bedroom window was third (barely, because I spent more time in bed than out).

Reading was fourth (but waiting for the time when it would vault over the front-runners) and—let me see—yes, peeing in the jar under my bed came next. My age at that time was seven, maybe six. I remember little or nothing before then. My sisters had their stories, told to me when I was an adult, but I had to take them on trust.

No mental prodding was required to recall those early books. I can still see the covers, remember the smell of the smacking new ones brought to my bed by relatives. *Bomba, the Jungle Boy, The Flying Aces* of *World War I, The Hardy Boys,* of course, and *The Lone Ranger,* a regular pal from the radio. And many that I will not list, since I know I am going to list others from years that followed.

Also referred to in the first volume of this anecdotal memoir is the book that opened the door to—literature. *Good* books. *Great* books. Books that sealed the deal on my contract with the written word for the rest of my days—years—life. I should mention another motivating factor: the mental picture of my father, sitting in his living room chair, pipe in mouth and book in hand. A regular routine, an indelible picture. He looked so satisfied in that setting. I said to myself, 'There must be something wonderful about reading, that he can be that happy.' Or words to that effect. My father wasn't always happy, though he tried to act as if he were. What I saw while he was reading was no act.

Back to my doorway to literature. On the other side of the door was, to begin with, *Huckleberry Finn.* Of all people to introduce him to me, the least likely to do so was my father's brother, the family black sheep. A kind and loving man who doted on his nieces and nephews (he had no children of his own). He had acted more in character when he'd taken me to Stillman's Gym in New York to have a fighter he knew teach me how to box—to "even some scores" on the street, as he put. That he introduced me to Rocky Graziano figured. That he introduced me to Huck did not. I thanked the fates and my uncle for both introductions.

Uncle Ben came to my bedroom and handed me the book during one of his visits. There were no words accompanying his gesture, such as "You'll like this." (How would he know?) "I enjoyed this book when I read it." (He hadn't.) Nor was a more likely comment offered. (Such as, "I don't what the hell this is all about, but here it is.") I reached out and thanked him. That was it.

Until I finished it. And read it again. The next time I saw him I thanked him profusely. He smiled and shrugged his shoulders and messed my hair. Unbelievable as it seems in retrospect, he never gave me another book. He did not have to; one was enough. *That* one hit the jackpot. The wonder and complexity of Huck's life, one with which I could not have fathomed, startled me into a determination to expand my elastic days into a sensory life. To get my baby ass out of bed once and evermore. (It took a visit to a 'quack doctor'—the AMA's term—in Biloxi, Mississippi and a year's effort.)

My father, well aware of the gift and my reaction, upgraded the reading matter that came to me from then on. He had me reading Lincoln (by and about Abe), Darrow (same as with Lincoln) and a few books by Sholem Asch (*Mary, The Apostle, East River*). "Starters," my father had said. But Huck really claimed that title.

Gifts from others expanded the new program. Hell, books made it even more important for me to get my next breath. Books, baseball and music (I will not include peeing as a pastime). They were my life. My lifeline. And, along with a limited number of other interests and devotions (baseball is *not* a devotion), they remain my "circumstances" and, as Gasset suggested, they go a long way in defining my self.

I do not have inspirational 'heroes' to point to as I think back on my life. Labels, as I have written, have always been suspect to me. But singular acts of particular people have 'pressed' (an inadvertent pun) on my being. Gutenberg, for one. Johannes Gensefleisch zur Laden zum Gutenberg holds a place of prominence on my list of life-favors (savers?) granted to me.

The man I referred to as 'Big John' apparently remains a very significant figure in the public domain. I had doubted that mass man gave him much thought. Or gave a tinker's damn about what he did. Yet, the A&E Network ranked him at the top of their list of "People of the Millennium." That was ten years or so ago. And a few years prior, *Time-Life* magazine selected Gutenberg's invention as the most important of the second millennium. Speaking for myself, his influence has been even greater than Rocky Graziano's knockout of Tony Zale.

The printing press. There, I finally got around to identifying Gutenberg's great achievement. That epochal invention, a way to mass-produce movable type, changed the limited production of books from handwritten manuscript to the revolutionary method of mass-producing books, books, books. The Renaissance blossomed due to this advance. I may not have blossomed (even yet) but my life has certainly been enhanced significantly by BJ's epiphany. Do I stand alone as beneficiary of his discovery? Of course not, but as Helen Keller said, no matter how many people share a good experience, each man thinks it was meant exclusively for his happiness. (Something like that.)

OK, so I am indebted to Big John. It was relatively easy to name favorite ball players, but how can I possibly provide a comprehensive list of favorite books? I can't. So let me muck my way through my mind and see what can be found there. Immediately, I find John Fowles. He's easy to spot: my very favorite writer. He wrote nineteen books, as far as I can tell. I think that's an accurate number. I have read sixteen of them. The three I have not 'caught up with' are about the place he lived in England: Lyme Regis. Two of them, at least. (The third is entitled, *Land*.) I will not catch up with them because I will not chase them. No interest.

I have a list of favorite books I keep—ever revised. This list includes fiction exclusively—literature. I certainly appreciate and read biography and history. Some philosophy, though I probably over-extended myself with it when I was a young man. Favorites of mine are the beautifully written and affecting autobiographical works of my friend, Frederick Buechner. No politics, no religion (some consider all of Fred's books to be 'religious;' I do not), no perceived contrived current crises or profundities of opinion by celebrities or other nobodies.)

So, to this list: Number One is a constant. It is there because it introduced literature to me. *Huckleberry Finn* is and will remain at the top. The other constant is Number Two: *The Magus* by Fowles. It opened doors in my mind to an elusive vastness that I still try to embrace. I recommended the book to a good friend many years ago. (Say, fifty years?) He read it. And read it again. And again. Needless to say, he loved it, as I did. But he has taken that love farther than I have or could have. He reads it again *every year*.

A scenario I can die with: I am resting comfortably on my death bed as Jerry Pesther recites *The Magus* to me. (I do not ask him to hold my hand.) He finishes the recital by translating from the Latin the author's final note, alluding to the character Nicolas Urfe—and to us all. "May each of us, who never loved before and may he who has loved, love tomorrow." Then Jerry is quiet, and, as Fowles has written, his "silence is a poem." And mine is a farewell.

Fowles had the chutzpah to write "a revised version" of *The Magus* twelve years after he had written the original. Why? He said he wanted to make the book more complete and satisfying—to him. "The basic principle of life is hazard," Fowles believed, but he also took control of whatever was possible to control—without any consideration of 'public opinion.'

What was assuredly less satisfying to him was the film version of *The Magus*, which appeared in 1968. I cringed when I saw it; it was a revoltingly terrible 'rendition' of the novel. A failure artistically, contextually—"totally," as my grandsons would say. Woody Allen was once asked if he would change anything in his life, if he could do so. He said he would do "exactly the same, with the exception of watching *The Magus*."

I am compelled to mention Fowles' *The Aristos*, a book of philosophy that has had a profound influence on my own thought. (I gave a copy to Fred Buechner many years ago, and as we stood in my Vermont kitchen, he indicated politely that it did not speak to him. I was not surprised. Nothing ventured. . . . We try to have friends like what we like.)

One minor piece of thought from the book must be noted here, because it relates to much of my life's work and because it is a bit of philosophy lost in the current societal fanaticism (from which the word 'fan' derives) that is disturbing to me. Said Fowles (forty-five years ago): "Sport is an opportunity for personal pleasure. (Pindar thought so 2,500 years before Fowles), a situation where beauty may arise. But what is being contested is never prestige. ('We're number one!?') Simply the game. (From Fowles' pen to sports fans' deaf ears.) The winner has more skill or more luck (amen); by winning he is not in any sense in any game necessarily a better human being than the loser."

This is not as profound as, for example, when he speaks of 'the anxiety of the ignorance of the meaning of life,' but what the hell, it is relevant commentary on what is seen and heard in stadium stands, newspapers and on ESPN. Annoying but ever-present parts of my professional life

I'm stuck on Fowles, it seems. Not stuck—attached. His one book of poems was interesting, if not wonderful in my view. But one poem, "The Picts," spoke directly to my feelings many years ago. The Picts were part of a collection of tribes in Northern Scotland, around the time before the Romans conquered Britain—until the 10th century. The title's connection to the context of the poem is made in the last line, "And then, like Hadrian, you build the Wall."

The Roman, Hadrian, was the third of the so-called "Five Good Emperors." His intention was to set off for Britain and have a wall constructed—a military barrier – to separate the barbarians from Romans. Eighty miles worth of wall.

The poem deals with the wall Fowles believes must eventually be built between old friends and oneself. ("One knows them more and more / And suddenly too much.") I had built such a wall, and the poem helped me justify my actions. I dismantled it, (not the entire length, to be honest) shortly after the one in Berlin had come down.

I used to read poetry frequently, especially when I was teaching literature. Not contemporary works, though I know much of it is very fine. My partiality was for the poems of Emily Dickinson, at the top of *that* list. Her line about fear—"zero at the bone"—I use frequently with athletes, who understand her metaphor exactly.

Auden's *"Musee des Beaux Arts"* speaks of the Old Masters' understanding of the suffering's human position. ". . . how it takes place / While someone else is eating or opening a window or just walking dully along." The poet refers to Brueghel's painting, "Icarus." In the painting, Auden says, "everything turns away / Quite leisurely from the disaster. . ." Turns away from Icarus, who flying too close to the sun, had his wax wings melt, and who, in the painting, falls into the sea (now named after him).

A ploughman "may have heard the splash, the forsaken cry, / But for him it was not an important failure." He had had things to do. The indifference is not a cruel one; it is a human. A ship "must have seen / Something amazing, a boy falling out of the sky." But it had "somewhere to get to and sailed calmly on."

I sail frantically back to my thoughts about the list of favorite fiction. I will allow myself to name what is, at this time (it is revised semi-annually), the top twenty-two. (The list has 40. Why 22? I just could not make it the Top Twenty, and leave off the next three. In consideration for the reader, I restrained myself from further inclusions.) Here they are, for whatever this may mean to anyone but me.

1) *Huckleberry Finn*, Mark Twain
2) *The Magus*, John Fowles
3) *Hopeful Monsters*, Nicholas Mosley
4) "The Alexandria Quartet," Lawrence Durrell
5) *Look Homeward, Angel*, Thomas Wolfe
6) *The Dream of Scipio*, Ian McEwan
7) *The Adventures of Augie March*, Saul Bellow
8) "The Deptford Trilogy," Robertson Davies
9) "The Regeneration Trilogy," Pat Barker
10) "The Avignon Quintet," Lawrence Durrell
11) *Birdsong Trilogy*, Sebastian Faulkes
12) *The Magic Mountain*, Thomas Mann
13) *Henderson the Rain King*, Saul Bellow
14) *Daniel Martin*, John Fowles
15) *All the King's Men*, Robert Penn Warren
16) *The Discovery of Heaven*, Harry Mulisch
17) *The Fires of Spring*, James Michener
18) *Blue*, Benjamin Zucker
19) "The American Empire Novels," Gore Vidal
20) *Time Will Darken It*, William Maxwell
21) *A Place of Greater Safety*, Hilary Mantel
22) "The Ægypt Cycle," John Crowley

I do not really appreciate James Michener's body of works in various geographical settings. But his coming-of-age, autobiographically inspired *The*

Fires of Spring (17) was a treat for me. As was Bellow's (whose entire body of work I have read and appreciated) *The Adventures of Augie March* (7), of the same genre as Michener's novel.

About ten years ago, I casually picked up a book by the Swedish writer, Henning Mankell. Since then, I have read everything he has written, in his understated but direct novels, most of them called 'police procedurals.' I had not read such books before, but in deference to my Swedish wife, and an interest in his theme ("What's gone wrong in Sweden?") I gave it a try. It opened up a door that led to Eric Ambler, who wrote espionage novels set in post World War I Europe. Ambler led me to Alan Furst, who then led me to Charles McCarry. Intelligent writers, all. A happy discovery.

For eighteen years I taught literature in Vermont. The works covered ranged from Steinbeck's *Of Mice and Men* to Dostoyevsky's *Crime and Punishment*. And poetry, of course. Also, the plays of Ibsen, Shaw, Arthur Miller and Shakespeare. My undergraduate English major allowed for exploration of many great works that influenced me and many reputedly great works that did not speak to me at all. I do not bother to list the so-called traditional classics that appealed to me, because they have spoken to the many, whereas those on the list of non-classical favorites above have spoken to the few. Fewer, at least. (Huck Finn is one of the few as a character, though the book has appealed to the many.) John Fowles has led me to care more for the few than the many.

Finally, I note a writer who was very important to me—and who, I believe, has been underrated by the literati: Somerset Maugham. He was rather prolific, writing such books as *Cakes and Ales, The Moon and Sixpence, The Razor's Edge* (his best novel, to my mind) *Of Human Bondage* (his most popular work). But his most affecting book—for me—was *The Summing Up*, an autobiographical work.

So much of what he said made sense to me when I read his words many years ago. They still do. Perhaps one line of his I have used more than any other in my life: "I find social intercourse fatiguing." Another favorite: "I have more character than brains; more brains than specific gifts." And, "I have loved individuals; I have never much cared for men in the mass." Here he vastly understates my own feelings on the subject of mass man. One more: "I have none of that engaging comehitherness that makes people take to one another on first acquaintance." I could have gotten on well with this man. I'm not as certain he would have taken to me.

Someone once said that books are the best furniture. Sister Dolly thought
so. She was an avid reader, but the quality of her choices left something to
be desired. She recognized this and did not apologize, nor should she have.
When she and her family moved into a new house with many bookshelves,
she assigned me the task of filling them up. I was initially excited. Then
she told me the requirements: they were all to be books published by The
Modern American Library (status symbol) and they had to have colorful
dust jackets (décor). Great. I loved my sister, not my task.

When Anita and I moved into our first house, we immediately found a
man who would craft built-in bookcases and form and arch over the wide
entrance to the living room. Pickled pine, I remember them to have been.
The shelf backings painted a blue to match the carpet. Décor again, but no
compromising of the books that would stand on the shelves. There was
much space initially, but gradually it diminished as the collection grew.
Furniture of our minds.

Each new house had more footage of shelf. One of Anita's nephew's
came to live with us for a while in Prescott, Arizona. When he arrived at
the house, he looked around and said, "Books, book, books." And hello to
you, John.

We moved to North Carolina sixteen years ago. One of the moving men,
who, with a companion, had finished lugging ninety-four cartons of books
into the house, wiped his brow—and said to my daughter-in-law, "He read
all these books?" She took it as a rhetorical question. But my answer could
be one I heard someone provide during a television interview. He said, "I
have read all of most, and some of all." In these books reside what has plea-
sured me over the years—and what, to a great extent, has defined me.

20

If

For reasons I will now share, I often have the two-letter word of the chapter's title running through my consciousness. I am not sure why it runs so insistently at *this time*. Perhaps the answer is that, because it has *always* been running—delivering its message to me, since the first delivery of my father's chastening of me when I was a boy—it is quickly brought to the surface at the least provocation. In this case, a late-night Billy Eckstine CD switched me on. He was singing "I Apologize." (The lyrics are referred to later in the chapter).

In the first volume of this trilogy, I noted what my father said to me after hearing an excuse pass over my lips. What I had thought of at the time as an explanation began with the words, "If only . . ." My father's rapid-fire response sped toward my ear—and lodged in my brain. Deep. "If frogs had wings, they wouldn't bump their asses on the ground," he said.

One good reason to write this seemingly frivolous chapter is to provide a segue between a chapter about books and another related to music. Besides, who needs an excuse for writing something in his own memoir? In any case, this bridge has some real meaning for me as I cross it.

When my father threw those frogs at me, I was shaken. The criticism, I knew, was valid. I was embarrassed and angry at the same time. But I do not remember making what I would determine to be an excuse ever again. Ever. Of course, someone else might think otherwise. And perhaps they'd be correct. So I will amend the statement: I never *consciously* made an excuse after that incident. What I made instead was a list. (I added to it as I approached the writing of this chapter.) The list was all about the word 'if.'

Some specific definitions—uses—should be established. Or *non*-uses. My major thrust is the word as a launching pad for excuses. I am not concerned about the word used to mean 'in the event that.' ("If the phone rings, answer it.") Or 'granting that.' ("If that's the case, you're fired.") Or 'on the condition that.' ("I'll let you use my ball if I can be the captain.") Or 'although possibly/even though.' ("She is an obnoxious if beautiful woman.") Or 'whether.' ("Find out if she thinks I'm hot.") Or expressing a wish or alternate possibility. ("If you had arrived earlier there would be dessert left for you to enjoy.")

But used in the context of an excuse? Well, that's another matter. *The* matter. ("If this infield wasn't horseshit, I would have made that play.") How many times have I heard athletes employing comparable 'if's'? Many. How many times have I heard another player respond to the excuse-maker (frogs notwithstanding) saying, "If wishes were horses then beggars would ride"? Many. It is part of the lexicon.

Many more times I have thought of the phrase, "For all sad words of tongue and pen / The saddest are 'What might have been.'" Words furnished by John Greenleaf Whittier. Hard copy by—who else?—Mac Dorfman.

And so, based on yet another lesson provided by a father who had a clue about dealing with a sick and callow son, I have gone through life listening to excuses and thanking him for not having to listen to me offering such weak—and sad—rationalizations.

Whittier actually wrote something else that affected me greatly. Said the poet, "No longer nor behind I look in hope or fear; / But grateful take the good I find / The best of now and here." Amen, brother. Amen, father.

Two or three years after the hypothetically winged frogs, my father presented another important poem to me. "Read this," he said in his direct, non-explanatory way. (He believed clarity was eventually arrived at without the need for elaborate preambles.) The poem was written by Rudyard Kipling. It's title: "If." Its message had a real and immediate (and sustained) influence on me. A photocopy of it is laminated and leaning against the fax machine on my desk. I have given a copy to many athletes—and, most recently, to a close relative. He was grateful and encouraged by it.

Especially by the opening words:

> "If you can keep your head when all about you
>   Are losing theirs and blaming it on you,
> If you can trust yourself when all men doubt you,
>   But make allowance for their doubting too;
> If you can wait and not be tired by waiting,
>   Or being lied about, don't deal in lies,
> Or being hated, don't give way to hating,
>   And yet don't look too good, nor talk too wise. . . ."

The final line of the poem, after all of Kipling's conditional prerequisites are stated, is "(Then) you'll be a Man, my son."

Last year, a bibliophile, a librarian and a loving daughter (all the same person) presented me with a copy of a what appeared to be (but isn't) a children's book. The text on the inside flap read: "What makes a boy into a man? . . . Courage, confidence, patience, integrity. . . . For more than one hundred years, this classic poem has inspired readers to reach for the best in themselves. In pictures and in words, here's what every boy needs to know most." All of this, I teach to the athletes I work with. All of this I have tried to enact myself, sometimes successfully.

Charles R. Smith, Jr. took the photographs of athletes performing in different sports. The photos accompany and illustrate each individual line of a poem. The poem is Kipling's. The book's title is, of course, is *If*. Leave it to Melissa to find a work that joined two subjects that were particularly germane to the existence of the recipient, her father.

The conditional 'if,' then, has also played a major role in my psychic world. After my father's introduction of flying frogs, my annoyance drove me to making a list. Since I was usually bed-ridden, I had the time and, then, the inclination for list-making. Mostly lists of 'favorites.' (See previous chapter.) Makes of cars, individual baseball players, aunts and uncles, strangers who passed regularly under my apartment window each day. ("He looks strong." "He looks kind." "She is beautiful." "She has a wonderful walk.")

But the list inspired by the little slimy, green, ass-bumping things (order, Anura; class Amphibia) was hooked to specific songs (as is the next chapter). It was about songs that have "If" as a title—or as the first word in the first line. I had meant it to justify (to myself) my own use of the word—after the insult of the hypothetical frogs. (I retained the list over the years, as I have done with some other personal detritus. No obvious reason; no excuse.)

A few titles have been added to the original. For example, a song sung by Sting. I never heard it, and I never want to hear it. But I heard *of* it, so it appears—providing proof of an old guy's contemporariness. (A reason, not an excuse.)

Now, I playfully present the list.

If You Knew Susie [like I know Susie] (sung by Eddie Cantor)
If You Were the Only Girl in the World (written in 1916 and sung by my
    father all through the 30's and 40's—as he moved through our apart-
    ment and, perhaps, in the bedroom)
If You Were Mine (Frankie Laine's jazz rendition)
If You Were Only Mine (1932 song revived in 40's by Buddy Clark, Don
    Cornell & Dick Haymes)
If (sung by Perry Como)
If I Loved You (Rogers & Hammerstein's *Carousel*)

If You Stubbed Your Toe on the Moon (Crooned by Bing Crosby; a
Jimmy Van Heusen movie tune. Tony Martin recorded it also.
If This Isn't Love (from *Finian's Rainbow*)
If I Didn't Care (Sung by the Inkspots)
If You Love Me (Jane Froman & Ray Noble's Orchestra–1936)
If You Haven't Got Love (Written for the Gloria Swanson film *Indis-
creet.*)
If I Ruled the World (Tony Bennett's version. Is there any other?)
If There Is Someone Lovelier Than You
If You Are But a Dream (A touching Sinatra rendition.)
If You Could Read My Mind
If You Could See Her ('The Gorilla Song' from, "Cabaret.")
If You Go Away (Piaf?)
If You Knew What It Meant To Be Lonesome (A plaintive country music
appeal? Is there any other kind?)
If You've Got the Money [I've got the Time] (Revived by Willie Nelson
in 1976.)
If You Love Somebody Set Them Free (Sting in 1985.)

My very favorites: Perry Como's rendition of "If." As in, "If they made
me a king, I'd still be a slave to you." And so on. (A bit much in terms of
courtship and a real reach in terms of possibility.) Tony Bennett would
have every day be the first day of spring in "If I Ruled the World." (A reach
beyond a grasp.) And, "If You Could Read My Mind"? (Titillating thought.
That would be trouble.)

But I sway from my original purpose, which was not to examine these
songs further than their titles. (Such discourse comes in Chapter 21.) My
childish motive was to find as many examples of people who used the
word. I just wanted to say that I was not the only kid who said "if." I was
also saying, "Put that in your pipe, Dad." All the while making no distinction between conditional use and *excuse* use. What the hell, I was only
twelve years old. My maturity was out of joint—as was my nose.

Because I wish to encourage further awareness of the impact of the word
in our language, I provide a sampling of first lines of songs. Also, just for
the fun of it.

"If you ever need a friend, here I am . . ." (From the song "Friendship.")
"If I told a lie; if I made you cry. . ." ("I Apologize," and Billy Eckstine is
convincing.)
"If ever I should leave you. . ." ("Never Would I Leave You" from *Camelot*)

Eddie Fisher sang, "If I ever needed love, I need it now." (Don't we all?)
Enough. *More* than enough. I will stop now.

I do not sing to my athletes, but I certainly talk about the word "if" and its usage. I make clear to them the difference between an excuse and a valid reason. But the distinction is difficult for many to make. ("It's hard to see the picture when you're inside the frame," I tell them.) In their pressure-packed world, in their fishbowl existence, the instinct to protect themselves from criticism and disparaging media evaluations is a strong one. And so, much time is spent helping them understand that difference. And speak according to the understanding—and their responsibility to own up to a mistake and to shut up about what was not.

Shortstop Walt Weiss, learning to be the exemplar he eventually became, booted a ground ball during a particular game. When he came into the Oakland dugout, teammates decried the poor condition of the infield. Walt said nothing. There was strength in his silence. (When he broke his silence after the game, he said, "I'm paid to make that play.")

So it has been, my interest and search for that kind of strength.

The French have a proverb related to excuse-making: "With the help of an 'if' you might put Paris into a bottle." A lousy proverb, *if* a clear point. Thomas Fuller, who had enough opinions to fill Paris, *if* he had lived there, wrote that bad excuses are worse than none. He, apparently, had not recognized the difference between an excuse and a reason. But that was in 1732, before politicians on television could provide clear examples.

My older sisters, as well as my father, (I wrote this in the first volume) had also heard excuses from me. Dolly, trying to teach me to dance, responded to my frustration with, "If you can't dance well, you blame the slippery floor."

The greatest drawback of an excuse, aside from the terrible 'message' it conveys to others, is that it gets in the way of finding a remedy to the mistake. Denial is an obstacle for awareness, and awareness is the first step to solving a problem. Ben Franklin, who often took a good point to a questionable extreme, did so offering his emphatic generalization (the better to make his point, of course): "He that is good for making excuses, is seldom good for anything else." Calm down, Ben.

If denial is admission, as Lady Macbeth suggested, then an obvious excuse is a more obvious confession. *If* the excuse-maker could only realize this. Shakespeare: "Oftentimes excusing of a fault / Doth make the fault the worse by the excuse."

As for the writing of this chapter, the Devil made me do it.

21

. . . But the Melody Lingers On

Beethoven was a dreamer; I'm a rememberer. He composed; I listen—and recall.

Recall with a memory that is said to be a peculiar organ. And though a particular memory may seem to be random, it actually can be prodded into patterns by other senses. The auditory, for example. At this age, the organ of memory has been more active, as other organs have become less active.

Such activity was triggered a few nights ago, as I sat in bed with my headphones on, waiting to be lulled into sleepiness by still another CD of choice for still another night. This disk's title, "Placido & Itzhak: Together," refers to vocalist Domingo and violinist Perlman. The first number they do together is composer Enrico Toselli's "Serenata." Sleep did not come. Because my mind was stimulated—activated—by a melodic memory. I had listened to this CD fairly often, yet this occasion brought a unique response. A question: Why is this tune squirming around, trying to free itself?

And then—the very next day—I received an e-mail from a wonderful young woman, who had worked with the Florida Marlins at the same time I had been an employee. We have remained pals over the years. Laurie has visited us in North Carolina and is a regular e-mail correspondent. The one I just received had an attachment. I opened it. There it was: background music, the theme song for the old television series, "The Goldbergs," a comedy-drama radio broadcast from 1929 to 1946, adapted into a 1948 play entitled "Me and Molly"—and then later seen as a television situation comedy from 1949 until 1956. (In 1973 a musical version, *Molly*, premiered on Broadway.) The theme was Toselli's "Serenata"—set loose in my mind, and now destined for association forever. (So long as *that* organ is working, I mean.)

Off my mind goes again—this time gathering broader thoughts related to music, which has been a great part of my life, from childhood to—now. Where to begin? "Some to church repair / Not for the doctrine, but the music there." I have not joined Alexander Pope in church—for either. But I have found music everywhere else in my life. Now that I am most often at home again, the ease of having it is assuring.

It is not my intention to speak of music's meaning to me in any grandiose manner. A rememberer, that's all I am. As far as grandiosity is concerned, though I very much appreciate and enjoy classical music, I prefer Sondheim to Stravinsky. Actually, I prefer anyone to Stravinsky. So I have my tastes; they are what they are.

When I was that bed-ridden child long ago, I often listened to WQXR, the classical station radio station with its studio in the Times Building. I remember writing in the first segment of this trilogy about a high school pal visiting me in my apartment and, upon hearing classical music coming from my bedside Emerson, telling me to "turn on something with words." (Last year, the public radio station WNYC purchased WQXR from the *New York Times*. Another historic fixture unfixed. I am without words to describe my disappointment.)

But classical music is not the matter that makes up my musical memories. While it can inspire and elevate me, it does not have the specific life associations that other music has had in my life. For example, if someone says to me, "The assassination of JFK," I would respond, "I'm sitting in a barber's chair on Commack Road, two miles from my home. It's lunch time and the barber has the radio on. We're the only two in the shop and we're listening to the news of the shooting."

If someone says, Bach's "Arioso," I'll respond, "Beautiful; I love it." But if someone says, "Deep Purple," I'll say immediately, "One of my sister Anita's favorite songs. Larry Clinton's orchestra; vocal by Bea Wain. She married Andre Baruch. They became disk jockey and jockeyette for a late afternoon segment (two or three hours) on WMCA—55 on my radio dial. I think of my sister lovingly whenever I hear the song or the singer. And of Bea Wain and her husband. And of what I was going through in bed as a youngster as I listened to their program every afternoon.

Though, as I have suggested, I am fond of classical music, I have few such associations, with one notable exception. During my high school and college years, I would work at the haberdashery operated by my two brothers-in-law. The store was in Valley Stream, New York, and I helped them and my financial situation each year during Christmas breaks. Both of my sisters lived in that town with their families. (Their husbands were partners in the business.) I would sleep over at one of their houses. One of my responsibilities at the store during those 'festive' weeks was to change the recordings on the record player in the back room. A speaker blared the typical selections of seasonal music into the spacious store: Crosby singing "I'll be Home for Christmas," some chorus shouting, "Ding dong, ding dong, sweet silver bells, Christmas is near, bring on good cheer"—and such blather. "White Christmas," of course, and freaking jingling bells. Over and over. (But I was well paid.)

Surprise was a pre-25th gift. Among the 33's back there with all those cacophonic greetings of the season (I must include Burl Ives' jolly, holly crap) was an Isaac Stern recording: Mendelssohn's "Concerto in E Minor for Violin and Orchestra, Op. 64." I would go to the back room and put this record on the turntable a disproportionate number of times, in an attempt to maintain some level of sanity. Mine. Customers didn't notice; they were in the store for too short a duration. The proprietors and salesmen didn't notice; they just heard the music of the cash register. So whenever I hear that piece, I have a Pavlovian Christmas response. Part good, part bad.

Short pieces that qualify as 'classical' are among my very favorites, *sans* associations. Tchaikovsky's "None But the Lonely Heart," Kreisler's "Liebesleid," and his "The Old Refrain." Massenet's "Elégie" also is high on my chart. And Rachmaninoff's "Oh, Cease thy Singing, Maiden Fair." Last of the class (but not least): Bach's "Art Thou with Me" (*Bist du bei mir*). Nietzsche thought that life without such music life would be an error. He thought even God sings songs. Bach would agree.

But the many songs I 'sing' of seem to me to comprise a rambling list as I ready them for presentation on the page. The real intention is to present a collection of recollection—of songs that, for one reason or another, have mattered to me. Most would be (and have been) categorized as 'American Standards.'

These standards are being revived by more and more vocalists—including Willie Nelson. But the impetus for the revival can be credited to Linda Ronstadt and her boxed collection of records issued in 1986, entitled "Round Midnight." A CD, "For Sentimental Reasons," followed years later. (With a selection of songs from the original collection.)

My interest was grounded in the 'dawn of an era'—1905 – 1919. My father sang, whistled and hummed many of them, which is how I was introduced to that era's music. I noted a few of them in an earlier volume. I remember him as he sat at the breakfast table, reading the racing form in the *New York Daily Mirror* and whistling "Will You Love Me in December as You Do in May?" He always felt he had to sing "I Wonder Who's Kissing Her Now." He told me that if he spotted a woman who was not wearing a slip, he'd sing, "Wait Til the Sun Shines, Nellie." That was more believable than the story he told me about a horse that shrugged its 'shoulders' when my father berated it for the animal's poor performance. He claimed to have waved a losing win ticket in the horse's face as it headed back to the paddock. Right.

Some more light came from the shine of a harvest moon he sang about, but not enough, I would imagine, to reveal the slipless woman's form. And a number of Stephen Foster songs were heard on the victrola in the living room. I also heard many such songs on the victrola at the home of an aunt and uncle.

One of my mother's brothers fancied himself as a vaudevillian dancer (my father was better). He had wonderful records at his apartment. It was a twenty-minute bus ride away from where I lived. I recall visiting Uncle Sam and Aunt Kate only when I wanted to hear the collection they had. (They visited our apartment frequently.) Uncle Sam's favorite: "When Frances Dances With Me." His sister's name was Frances. My mother, that is. He would make her play it on the piano, whenever the opportunity arose. She played wonderfully, but was too shy for 'public performances.' (We did not have a piano in our apartment, so I only heard her play at another uncle's apartment.)

But—the American Standard Songbook was my prevailing thought. It is currently referred to as 'Great American Songbook' (so people could conveniently call it GAS?). The big hitters (composers) are listed alphabetically: Arlen, Berlin, Carmichael, Ellington, the Gershwins, Kern, Mercer, Porter, Rogers and Hart, Rogers and Hammerstein and Jimmy Van Heusen (whose "But Beautiful" was even recorded by Kenny Rogers, though other renditions—especially Rosemary Clooney's—are far superior.)

The Songbook includes the music of Broadway and tunes from Hollywood musicals, (so many memorable, incomparable songs)—and those of the famous Tin Pan Alley, where the offices of almost all the agencies for composers and their songs were located. There, the enduring music of the 20's—through, let's say—the 60's, was auditioned, accepted and sent into the outer space of recordings, radios and, later, juke boxes.

WNEW in New York was one home for all the songs of these composers. The pointer on my radio dial was fixed on 1130 every day, as I sat in my sickbed. When I was reading, the volume was dialed down. But I heard. Years of that radio music and the singing of family members went into my ears and stayed in my head.

Scene: I am having a bad day. Deep breaths are at a premium. Reading is not possible. My sister, Dolly, comes home from work. She sits at bedside and sings, "Let's Be Buddies." (Cole Porter) I manage a smile. Every time I play the CD with Ethel Merman singing that song with an eight-year-old named Joan Carroll (from the musical, *Panama Hattie*) I manage another smile. Or just when I think of it, as I do now.

My sister Anita did not sing to me as often as Dolly. (Maybe because she once forgot the words as she sang a song with Dolly on Sunday radio's "Horn and Hardart Children's Hour"?) But a favorite of hers—and it too was meant to distract and please her little brother—was "My Buddy" (lyrics by Gus Kahn and music by Walter Donaldson—the first of more than 100 songs written by that team). ". . . I think about you all through the day / My buddy, my buddy, your buddy misses you." Doris Day couldn't sing it better, though she tried in a 1951 movie about Kahn's life.

When Frank Sinatra did live performances, he always gave credit to the composer of the work he was about to sing. Tony Bennett does the same, honoring the person who was responsible for birthing the song. For example, Sinatra would introduce a presentation by saying, "This next song of love and devotion is called 'If There is Someone Lovelier Than You' and was written by a gentleman who had many other lovely songs to his credit, Arthur Schwartz."

Arthur Schwartz did write many other wonderful songs but, because he was not Berlin or Kern or Hammerstein, the acknowledgement he got from Joe and Jane Listener was nearly non-existent. Those in the business knew all about him—and about many like him. I have therefore committed myself to list a few less-known (some little known; others virtually unknown) composers and their famous music. Just a few? Well . . .

ARTHUR SCHWARTZ:
   Dancing in the Dark (I can think of no one else but Fred Astaire singing it.)
   You and the Night and the Music (I liked Tony Martin; I appreciated his wife, Cyd Charisse even more.)
   Something to Remember You By (The first time I heard it, Polly Bergen was the artist.)
   I Guess I'll Have to Change My Plans (Sinatra, good; Mel Tormé, better.)

WALTER DONALDSON: (previously mentioned):
   Yes Sir, That's My Baby (Eddie Cantor launched it.)
   My Blue Heaven (I have a few copies of old sheet music for a number of great oldies framed and hanging on a wall—and one artist is the guy who sang this song, Gene Austin.)
   My Mammy (Did anyone even *try* to sing it after Jolson?)

SAMMY FAIN:
   You Brought a New Kind of Love to Me (Rendered by the incomparable Maurice Chevalier.)
   That Old Feeling (My favorite treatment comes from the same album/CD mentioned in the previous chapter—"Jazz Spectacular" with Frankie Laine.)
   I'll Be Seeing You (So many sang this WW II classic.)
   I Can Dream, Can't I? (My personal Fain favorite, sung by the Andrew Sisters.)

DOROTHY FIELDS: (Yes, a woman!)
   I Can't Give You Anything But Love (Figures?)
   I'm in the Mood for Love (More love!)
   Make the Man Love Me (A pattern here)
   Don't Blame Me (Nat 'King' Cole makes it a man's tune.)
   If My Friends Could See Me Now (A show-stopper from the Broadway
      musical, "Sweet Charity, with Gwen Verdon knocking it out—and left
      off the 'If list' so I could save it for now.)

E.Y. ('Yip') YARBURG: (Probably better known that most of the others
listed)
   When I'm Not Near the Girl I Love (He wrote others that were wonderful
      and also part of the score for "Finian's Rainbow.")
   How Are Things in Glocca Morra? (As noted above.)
   April in Paris (Doris Day did it first, but I kept playing a better rendition
      on a jukebox in a bar in Brockport, New York, during my grad school
      days. A widely popular instrumental treatment by Count Basie that
      endures.)

RALPH RAINGER:
   Thanks for the Memory (Introduced in Bob Hope's film debut in 1938,
      Hope sang it with Shirley Ross and the song was an Academy Award
      winner. Not the movie or the actors.)
   I Wished on the Moon (I hear Billie Holiday's plaintive offering as I write
      this.)
   Please (Crosby introduced it in a 1932 film and its popularity spread af-
      ter he recorded it—Al Hibbler and Giselle MacKenzie tried many years
      later.—Please.)
   June in January (Crosby again.)
   Love in Bloom (More Crosby—but this became Jack Benny's theme song
      and he played it—well, terribly—on purpose.)

HARRY WARREN: (This guy deserves to be spoken of in the same breath
with the 'big boys.')
   Lullaby of Broadway (Sung by virtually everyone)
   Chattanooga Choo Choo (Glenn Miller with Tex Beneke and the Mod-
      ernaires
   Serenade in Blue (Another song that Glen Miller, this time with Ray Eb-
      erle as vocalist)
   The More I See You (Dick Haymes, who also sang one of my very favorite
      songs—though not by Warren—"Stella By Starlight.")
   I Had the Craziest Dream (Harry James, the guy who turned my boyhood
      fantasy world upside down by marrying Betty Grable, nevertheless
      does a fine job on his trumpet. The vocalist, Helen Forrest.)

This Heart of Mine (Sinatra, convincingly.)
You'll Never Know (Even more convincingly.)
I Want to be a Dancing Man (Fred Astaire, surprise.)
You're Getting to be a Habit with Me (Funny thing, Maureen McGovern
   scores at the top for me on this one.)
An Affair to Remember (Considered by many to be the most romantic
   film ever made, it had Vic Damone singing the theme with the opening
   credits. Deborah Kerr 'sang' [dubbed voice] at the tearful end.)

KURT WEILL: (I had to include him because of . . .):
September Song (Walter Houston, who else?)
Mack the Knife (I'm happy to end the list with a song I find to be quite
   irritating.)

Others are unstated but not unappreciated. But lines must always be
drawn and my tired mind has determined the time to be now, though I
wish, as Perry Como (and the Fontaine Sisters) said in *The Alphabet Song,*
"I could go on all day."

It was only a few years ago that I discovered that Arthur Schwartz was the
father of one Jonathan Schwartz, musician, club singer and—best known to
me—a disk jockey on WNEW during its final years. The son, a Sinatra aficionado and devotee, would host Saturday Sinatra segments and gush over
the qualities of renditions offered by "Old Blue Eyes." So what? So be it.

Our family's involvement in music (two singing sisters, a mother who
occasionally played piano during showings of silent movies, a father
who fancied himself to be an amateur vaudevillian—and me with two
ears—though I did sing in the high school chorus until I decide it wasn't
cool—fool) expanded when sister Anita married a professional singer. (I
was eight at the time.) Frank Borden was a baritone with a widely acknowledged beautiful voice. The standard tough-luck cliché applied to him and
his career: he never got *the* big break. (That's why he eventually ended up
partnering in a men's wear store with sister Dolly's husband.)

He sang in clubs (Havana, Miami, New York, Jersey, California) and at
resorts in the Catskill Mountains. For a time, he had a radio show: fifteen
minutes in the evening—on WHN in New York. He had two theme songs
for that program, one to open it and one to close. The opener was "My
Song" and the closer was "We'll Meet Again." Frank also made a short film.
He played a singing (one song) train conductor. It was a ridiculous flick;
the impression was so bad, I forgot what he sang.

He also competed for a spot on Arthur Godfrey's radio program. The
competition—a tryout, so to speak—included the performer and his or
her child. Frank brought his only child, Bonnie. She sang with clarity but

without inspiration. The other finalist had a son who was a knockout, so the father beat Frank out.

The winner played—the musical saw. What the hell! That is the polite reaction of my dentist/mentor/sparring partner/family friend, Al Roses. We were both listening in his office. "That," he concluded, "was a goddam shame." It was. Many people in the business compared Frank's voice favorably to that of Robert Merrill. I have a couple of tapes from his radio broadcasts. Though his voice was powerful, his career was relatively weak. He did very well as a haberdasher.

His voice and repertoire left strong impressions on my musical tastes. His songbook was diverse: classical, semi-classical (opera and operetta music included in that category) and some contemporary. (His selection for the losing Godfrey competition was "Smile.") Live audiences at his club and resort performances always requested what became (to his dismay) his 'signature song': "The Donkey Serenade." (Alan Jones had been there first with that one.)

With Frank's influence, I bought 78 (rpm) and, later, 33 1/3 recordings of John Charles Thomas, Enrico Caruso, Robert Merrill, Jan Peerce, Richard Tucker, Jussi Bjoerling and Paul Robeson. Even Mario Lanza and, as the record jacket says, "Our Man from Italy"—Sergio Franco. (His best was *I' Te Vurria Vasá*—"I Want to Kiss You.")

All of these I now have on CD's, (except Franco) to accompany Domingo, Pavarotti, Carreras, Bryn Terfel, Andrea Bocelli—and an interesting new guy, Paul Potts. (The sparrow voices of Irish tenors I can do without.) For the gender record, so to speak, I also have recordings of Callas, Sutherland, Sills, Fleming, Von Stade and Battle. Oh yes, and Lotte Lehmann.

I enjoy jazz, though I am discriminating about what I listen to. Gene Ammons on tenor sax ("The Gentle Jug") is one of the most beautiful musical experiences I have had—and continue to have) But the pervasive interest and pleasure for me has been the music that emanated from Tin Pan Alley. Though special songs have camped in the tents of my mind over the years, I will let them rest for the time being. Enough lists. I feel like belting out "I Feel a Song Coming On" (Dorothy Fields, sung by Alice Fay, wife of bandleader Phil Harris in a 1935 film), but that would lead to another list. I would not be able to restrain myself once I started.

Using that restraint, I will say, as Berlin said before me, the song has ended—but the melody lingers on. And the memories provoked by all those early songs. The many memories.

22

Diamond Dustings

"Women and elephants never forget," said the sharp-witted writer, Dorothy Parker. I am neither a member of the female gender nor of the order Proboscidea. But there are particular and varied baseball recollections settled like dust into the softness of my soft brain. I must speak of them, for no other reasons than to have them provide some final examples of people who crossed my path as I walked my hundreds of miles through twenty-six years on and off baseball diamonds. Heading toward old age I try to convince myself that Montaigne was not referring to me when he said that a strong memory "is commonly coupled with infirm judgment." *Que sera, sera.*

Fame is a magnifying glass. Many players I have come in contact with achieved public recognition. Many more—those who worked so hard as minor leaguers—failed to reach their goal and never became part of the collective conscientiousness of baseball fans. When the dust settles on baseball diamonds across the country, they are nowhere to be found, even with a spy glass. But I remember most of them. Some fondly, some not. Some clearly, some not. Some with amusement, some with sadness. But they are there in my consciousness, at varying levels, to be sure.

A few have particular significance because many of the themes they offered have been somewhat instructive. At least, they are very clear and accessible. The themes and their representative experiences follow.

WHEN IT MATTERS TOO MUCH. One of the greatest obstacles athletes (people!) set up for themselves is adopting the perspective that some situation they face is 'life or death.' I often ask players to imagine a three-foot wide plank running across the room in which we sit. "If I asked you to walk across this plank, you'd give me a funny look, get on the plank, skip and do a pirouette, and get to the end of it with a grin." The player usually nods in affirmation. "But if we put same kind of plank across Grand Canyon, your attitude and behavior—your perspective—will be entirely different. And so will your muscles. Your legs will lock up; you won't be able to move. That is a life or death situation. Playing baseball is not—unless you determine it to be that." And so on.

One illustration: I was standing on line at a Burger King in Birmingham, Alabama. The Double-A team I was spending time with was en route home to Huntsville now that the nine road games had been completed. The bus had stopped so the players could get something (greasy) to eat. In front of me stood a pitcher who had been playing for a good number of years; no youngster, as minor leaguers go.

Russ turned around to me and said, "You know, Harv, I think this is it for me (in pro ball). I'm going home. My wife is teaching and I have a great offer to work for UPS. Good pay, good benefits."

Russ had been ineffective as a starting pitcher and he was moved to the bullpen, where matters did not improve. He always put excessive pressure on himself, as many do. I responded, "Russ, it's the beginning of August. One month to go. Wait until the end of the month (when the minor league season ended) and evaluate the situation then." His silence betokened consent.

What happened to his performance was astounding—to him. He pitched magnificently. I returned to that team as the season ended. I asked Russ if he knew what happened. He was not an innocent young kid. "Yeah, I know," he said with a small smile. "I had nothing to lose anymore. I had a job waiting for me at home and I had decided the end (of his baseball career) had come. So I pitched free and easy. It didn't matter. It sure as hell wasn't life or death anymore."

Overbearing didact that I am, I had to say, "It never really was."

Russ, having learned directly from his experience, rather than vicariously (from my group and individual talks), pitched respectably for another five years. He reached Triple-A but never the major leagues. His limited talent was the reason, not his perspective, which had expanded. He appreciated and enjoyed pitching, after his acquired insight. He appreciated himself.

What matters is how a person approaches his task. If it matters too much, he will think about possible 'catastrophic' consequences. The focus on will be on failure. On feelings, not function.

"TELL ME HOW YOU REALLY FEEL." This is a line players use all the time when someone 'goes off' in his expression of a strong, often heavy-handed, opinion or feeling related to a situation or another person. The remark is an ironic one, of course. Another way of saying, "You're being rather aggressive here."

Matt Sinatro is currently the first base coach for the Chicago Cubs. For years, he has been called Lou Piniella's "caddie" because the Cubs manager has taken him wherever he's gone. They started together when Sinatro was still a player, in Seattle. I met Matt when he was at the Oakland spring training camp in 1987, trying to catch on with our major league team after two previous years in the minors. He had originally signed with the Atlanta Braves, playing (part-time) for them from 1981 to 1984. A second-round draft choice of the Braves, he never really panned out.

A mutual acquaintance called me recently to tell me he ran into Matt and my name came up. Said the fellow on the phone with me, "He told me how he was introduced to you." I did not recall immediately. Until the person on the other end of the phone set the scene.

"Matt said he was taking part in an infield drill you were watching. (Sinatro was a catcher.) He screwed up a couple of times, he said. After the drill, he got some water and came up to you and started talking about the screw-ups."

The person on the phone then told me "exactly what Sinatro said" about that first meeting.

Sinatro speaking: "I mean, I'd never met the guy. I knew who he was and all, but I didn't know him. So I start talking and, after a few sentences, he puts up his hand (palm facing him, one of my tendencies, like a cop stopping traffic) and says, 'Let me ask you something. Do you always make excuses?' I mean I never met the guy. I found out later he does that to everyone. Pretty funny."

Not "to everyone." But Matt, at least, got the message, and he put a harness on what had been a runaway instinct for ass-covering.

He played two years in the Braves organization, one with the Tigers and finished with Seattle, where he accompanied his manager on the golf course and elsewhere. We had a number of happy reunions since my question was asked that day.

LEOPARDS DON'T CHANGE THEIR SPOTS. This is a line a manager once dropped on me when he was trying to make the point that I was wasting my time with a player people projected as having 'no chance' of becoming a major league player. That kind of projection is one frequently offered by evaluators of players. That particular line has been expressed occasionally but embraced regularly.

Two players, both pitchers, come to mind immediately. I will expand on one and mention the other. The young high school and college draftees had been signed and reported to Oakland's rookie orientation program in Medford, Oregon. I was always there for the beginning of that program.

On the first day I was standing near the stands behind home plate, where the kids would sit and listen to all the staff members telling them what should be done and how to do it. Naturally, I was one of the presenters. The players straggled out of the clubhouse. One walked down the third base line toward home plate—and me.

"You're an asthmatic?" I said quietly to him as he came near me. He asked me how I knew that. "The way you're holding your shoulders up—the better to get air. Today's a bit tense for you, I'd guess—and you're breathing is affected."

His tension, I would find out in the shower room, also manifested itself in other ways; nasty boils spread across his back—and halting, uncertain speech. Not quite a nervous stutter, but no fluidity or continuity at all. He would have social difficulties because players, being human (not a compliment here), teased, ridiculed and ostracized him. He was a mess. The staff immediately decided he had no chance for success.

Surprisingly, he had some resilience and at that lower level of competition, he 'hung on.' I spent an inordinate amount of time with him—for one simple reason: he needed it. I was concerned about his social survival as well as his future in professional ball. Hence, the leopard reference. The theory, based on cynicism rather than intelligence and information, still prevails because the laws of probability are against such a player.

But the statistics are against *every* player. Out of 100 players who sign a professional contract, anywhere from seven to fourteen get to be major leaguers. Even first round draft choices are vulnerable to this truth.

So what chance did this kid have, the staff asked in their statistical mind? Without intervention, very, very little (I refuse to say 'none'). With intervention—guidance, encouragement, support, instruction, optimism and so on—some chance. In this case, the pitcher matured, improved his physical condition—because he improved his mental condition—and pitched in the major leagues for ten years.

The other pitcher, a first round choice who the staff disparaged because the prevailing pundits said, "He's a pussy." Another label. Yes, his *behavior* was soft, but he did not *want* to be that way. He and I had a wonderful love/hate relationship. He hated me when I made him be honest with himself. He loved me when he succeeded. He became a man and pitched in the big leagues for sixteen years. Sixteen!

At a spring training game, a veteran catcher pal of mine who had been with Oakland when this player, now a veteran, was being disparaged, greeted me and said, "You'd be proud of your boy. The manager's afraid of him." The manager had a reputation of being a 'tough guy.' The player, referred to in later days as a 'bulldog,' had changed, apparently, from feline to canine.

People can change if they do something about their situation and themselves. Wanting to change is a start, but the insistent will I continually speak of is required. As is a little help along the way. Even with some assistance, it is a very difficult process, to say the very least. But it can be achieved, simply because—we are not leopards—or pussies or bulldogs. We can be many things, but our *acts* reflect our tendency of the moment. So I may act cowardly in one setting and bravely in another. Labels, ach.

ONE-EYED CAT. This is the name of a game/conditioning exercise for pitchers. At least it used to be when I was at the Oakland A's spring training camp. Pitchers have some fun as they get their running in. They love to hit, especially American League pitchers, who have others designated to hit for them. This drill gives them a chance to swing and run and trash talk and have a helluva good time.

A coach at the camp throws from the mound to the two teams comprised of pitchers. They hit the ball, run straight to second base, which acts as the first base of regular games. The next base in home plate. So they are running back and forth and getting their exercise. There is no stopping in between: only outs or a runs scored. The rules of the game are irrelevant.

What was relevant was the fact that I was selected, on a particular day, to be the pitcher. The pitches are made from the front of the mound to spare coaches' old and tired arms. I decided to have fun for myself. I geared up and took my role 'seriously,' much to the delight of the players. My fastball was quite hittable, of course, but I mixed in breaking balls and changes in speed. The delight increased. "Harv's dealing," one of the players shouted. Plenty of fun.

Pitcher Jeff Musselman, who now runs the administrative office as a vice-president in the Scott Boras Corporation, and is a colleague of mine, stepped to the plate and promptly hit the first pitch over the left field fence. Hilarity. Smack-talking to and about the pitcher—me. The next hitter stepped into the box. They weren't going to get comfortable with me, I determined. Did I think I was Don Drysdale or Sal Maglie? No, I would just maintain the same approach I had when pitching in college, I said to myself proudly. (Every ass likes the sound of his braying.)

And then I *did* the same thing: I knocked the hitter, a fellow named Reggie Harris, on his butt with a pitch high and tight. Hilarity unbounded, this time aimed at the hitter. "He's gonna make you pay, Reggie!" Reggie refused to get back in the box. The mood was magnificent. They ran and talked and laughed their asses off.

To make peace, I took Reggie to dinner and a movie that night. I remember the film, which I never would have gone to see on my own. It was called "The Commitments" and had some good music in it. We both enjoyed it. I was not invited to be a participant again. The bemused word around the camp was, "Don't mess with Harv."

What's the point to this bit of trivial memory? That once in a while, work was a joy. (It was always interesting, usually rewarding, occasionally frustrating—rarely 'fun.')

THE BEST ARMOUR; THE WORST CLOAK. Thomas Fuller said that about the dogma of religion. I will let the words speak for themselves. I will speak about a few visitations experienced with religious enthusiasts.

While I was writing and teaching in Vermont, I became acquainted with and close to a wonderful baseball player and a more wonderful young man. His name is Dale Murphy. Dale was then an outfielder playing for the Atlanta Braves. It was evident he would be a fine player, and he did indeed become one. We first met in Montreal, where I covered visiting National League teams who came to play there (as well as the locals) for a Vermont newspaper. This was before I had started research for *The Mental Game of Baseball*.

I approached Dale during his team's batting practice and asked if he would consent to an interview. I told him I wanted to write an article about him for the Mormon magazine, *New Era*. Dale, of course, is a Mormon. He was happy to grant my request and said that a teammate of his, Barry Bonnell, was also a Mormon and he'd like Barry to be part of the story. I consented to that.

The article was written and appreciated by both players, and led to a friendship. After Barry was traded to Toronto, Dale and I would have lunch every time the Braves came to Atlanta. But before Barry was traded, the two of them double-teamed me at a luncheon and worked vigorously at converting me Mormonism. They were well versed on the sect's history, not so much on mine. I finally said, "Will you allow me to just remain who I am and still maintain this relationship?" Reluctantly, they agreed, after assuring me they were proselytizing for my own good—for their concern for me. "We like you, and we want you to be one of us," Dale said.

Another attempt to convert me was made a couple of years later, in Albany, New York, where I was now preparing for the book—and, unknowingly, for a change of careers. I had spent the better part of the summer of 1984 with the Albany A's, an Oakland farm team. Two players took me aside after a batting practice session. They were 'born again' Christians. The spokesman, an infielder name Thad Reece, told me that I should become "one of them." I told him that being born once was quite enough for me. He smiled politely but bore down, firing warnings at me related to my soul. Exasperated by my sardonic look, perhaps, he said. "You say the same things Jesus says, except that you swear when you're saying it." At that a smile appeared on my face.

"Let me ask you this," I said. "If I say all those good things and I do good things, as you say I do, will I not go to heaven?"

He said I would not, unless I turned myself over to Christ.

"So a very good person who doesn't turn to Christ will not go to heaven, but a not-so-good person who gives himself to Christ will go to heaven. Do I have that right?"

"Yes," he said, without further justification for this seeming discrepancy.

"Well," I said, quoting Mark Twain, "'It's heaven for climate and hell for society.' All my friends will be down there in the hot place." Thad and the other silent partner, a fellow whose last name (Lambert) is all I can recall, shook their heads in frustration and walked away. The subject never came up again. Pure logic is the ruin of the spirit.

Years later, the most dramatic religious experience I had in baseball took place at an Oakland minor league spring training camp. We had signed a young high school catcher, a controversial second-round draft choice. The controversy was based on the fact that many (most) did not think he had the physical tools to be selected that high in the draft. But the powers prevailed. As it turned out, he had neither the physical tools nor the mental traits required for success.

Talent (or lack of) aside, his mental makeup was not immediately apparent. His early days showed him to be a benign 'yes-man.' He wished to make no waves during his first experiences as a professional player—from his signing in June through the Instructional League program in October. But he brought a religious typhoon with him to spring training the following year.

William (I'll call him here) walked around camp with a face that looked as if he suffered from trigeminal neuralgia. Something was brewing under it. He became a pain in my ass. (Did I suffer from buttocksinal neuralgia?) His born-again zealotry created a perpetual intoxication—a fever of the mind. A boy who had hung on my every word when I spoke at rookie orientation and talks during Instructional League, William, his face now indicated—as he stood with the other players while I delivered what he now considered to be unholy daily blasphemes—was clearly annoyed and offended. He soon told the highest power (*I* mean the person running the camp) that my point of view violated him. What had put me over the top as a heathen was a talk I gave about will power: how important it is for players to have insistent wills as they prepared and approached their tasks on the field.

"God's will takes care of everything," he told me after the talk was completed. He told me that and more. It is not necessary for me to repeat it. It can be heard from any fundamentalist, anywhere. Quite the opposite of what is typical with young men, he had been a sober colt who became a wild horse. The other players considered him to be only the back end of a horse.

William complained about me to Karl Kuehl; he wanted my talks to cease. Karl said the best he could do was to excuse William from them. That was accepted with reluctance. His insistent will (I smile here) in the clubhouse began to irritate the other players. They went to Karl; William, reluctantly and petulantly, curtailed his proselytizing—except when he surreptitiously cornered someone he thought was not vehemently opposed to be saved.

Had William's rational mind been maligned by lack of use? Only God knows, and He surely has given *me* no hint of the answer. Whatever the case, William became more inclined to persecute than to persuade. Perhaps his zeal became (if it were ever anything else) a matter of prideful posturing rather than profound belief. Would his religion survive his moral makeup? Would he survive his religious fever? (Is God smiling?)

William did not survive his lack of talent or his talent to irritate. Oakland released him, with no reluctance. Disappointment, yes. We did not see him show up—as is the case with many castaways—in another team's camp. Perhaps he was setting up his own, so to speak.

WHAT'S FUN FOR SOME IS DEATH FOR OTHERS. Aesop wrote about frogs that provided a rock-throwing boy with this bit of truth. The boy understood. Not exactly parallel was a lesson learned by a minor league pitcher in the Florida Marlins camp. But close enough. I had watched carefully as this young man acted out the role of class clown. Even the manager made jokes about him in front of the other players. After all, the player seemed to *want* it. To want the attention.

After I had seen and heard enough, I called the player, Mike, into an office and told him what I thought: that he was covering his ass, his lack of confidence and self-esteem with this act. I went deeper with my analysis. When I had finished, he said to me, "How do you know all that?"

"Easy," I said. "That's what I did when I was a kid. The difference is, I was in junior high school. You are in your early adulthood—chronologically, at least. It's time for you to grow up. If you had taken yourself seriously, you still would be in the big leagues." (He had pitched briefly with the Pirates.) He said he was unburdened (I can't recall his exact word) and would be glad to change his presentation of self. I told him it would take time for others to get the new message he was bringing to camp each day.

I went to the manager and told him to back off. "No more jokes about this guy; take him seriously." Mike's behavior changed dramatically. So did his performance. He liked his new self, he told me. The story could have had an Aesopian ending, had a couple of things gone differently. But the Marlins acquired a pitcher in a trade and Mike became the last player cut at the end of the spring. The manager was as sad as the player, when he delivered the news to Mike. But he took it like a man, went down to Triple-A and pitched effectively.

But he never got back to the major leagues. He is now working for a very successful agent, whose name is *not* Scott Boras.

EINSTEIN STRIKES AGAIN. Because of the ever-evident sweat shirt on my back, the players refer to it as my "Einstein look." On occasion, my talks include one of his profundities about life. This has little direct meaning here, but it popped into my head because of what follows.

While I was with the Marlins, a players' strike was in progress. The fear of fans and ownership was that it would last, and the season would be lost. Management decided to take make a dramatic countervailing move: they brought in replacement players. 'Scabs,' in the vernacular of all striking workers, baseball players included.

So spring training was held, after all. Former major leaguers, guys who played in Japan or in college and never aroused interest from professional teams arrived in Melbourne, Florida, where we trained. All kinds of wannabees showed up at all big league camps. It was a farce. More like fantasy camps than major league training camps. Ours was no exception.

The thing was, they were good guys, and when the staff could suspend its initial aversion, disbelief and anxiety about a prolonged strike, we actually had fun. One particular player, a pitcher named Steve Firevoid, spent a lot of time talking with me about family, his job (in the financial field) and philosophy of life. He had an inquiring mind and an unformed self. He had pitched in five games for the San Diego Padres in 1981. His record was 0-1, but his earned run average had been a respectable 2.77. In any case, he was one who had much on his mind—and in it. He helped the time pass quickly.

And it did. By the end of the spring, word came that the strike was settled. The regular players would arrive and 'get ready' for the season during the few days that remained. Rene Lachmann, a jovial, fun-loving manager, scheduled a farewell dinner at the complex. After dessert had been demolished, he said that everyone in the room, would stand up—one at a time—and say something of significance related to their experience at the camp.

This was done. Some presentations were very amusing. Some were touching, heartfelt stories about appreciation for being treated so well by the staff and the opportunity to fulfill a dream. Etc.

My turn concluded the proceedings. I stood up, wearing my sweat shirt, of course, and said that a crazy thing had happened to me. I told the players, "You guys are so bad that the groupies hanging around the ballpark were approaching *me* with interest. In fact," I continued (borrowing from a story Einstein told), "the other afternoon that beautiful blond you might have seen sitting behind our dugout stopped me in the parking lot after the game. She told me she wanted to have my baby. 'I've heard about you,' she said. 'With my looks and your brains' we would have the perfect child.'"

I paused for effect, while the audience smiled and chuckled at the thought of such a scenario—and waited for me to continue. After my Jack-Benny-like pause, I went on. "I said to her, 'What happens if the kid ends up having my looks and your brains?' and got into my car and drove away."

"Einstein would have been smarter than that," one player shouted above the laughter. After final words from Lach, the party ended on that note of gaiety. As do my baseball stories.

23

Odds & Ending

"Baseball pulled my life into its orbit." A narrator of a television documentary said that. My own orbit has had many other influences. (His did also, probably.) Writer Nikos Kazantzakis wrote, "God makes us grubs, and we, by our own efforts, must become butterflies." Mixed metaphors aside, it is very apparent that books, music—and particular people—have also coaxed me out of my grubbiness. I do not think I qualify as a butterfly. A moth, perhaps?

My father insinuated himself into my life and remains there still. Insinuate: "to introduce by subtle or artful means." He employed both approaches. Yet his pull was strong and it determined, to a great extent, my orbital path. I hear myself referring to his wisdom every time I counsel someone—or write a chapter in this book. I am reminded of Pat Conroy's description of one of his fictional characters, calling the man more of "a North Star" than a father. That could describe Mac Dorfman, as well.

So now, having followed that star and orbited through all else that has happened to me, I am here, wherever that is and whoever I am. No metaphor necessary.

The interest my daughter, Melissa, had in having me write this trilogy, was to allow my grandsons, as she stated it, "to know who their grandfather is." I have done the writing. The interpretation is their business—and that of any others who may care to paint their individual mental pictures of me, for whatever purpose that would serve. I will make a last attempt at being helpful—for the sake of those three boys—by devoting this final chapter to ideas, intentions and other matters that have been important to me, for better or for worse. And that may provide a final, specific glimpse at what I concern myself with. I am happy to say it falls far short of self-revelation.

I know the world is complex, and so are humans. All the more reason to try to cut through all the bullshit without and within. This, I believe, Somerset Maugham tried to do. He set a good example for me. I *know* it is what I have tried to do. Sometimes I've been successful; other times less so. I can recall a couple of times I failed miserably to keep my eye on the ball (as I remind all the hitters I work with).

Simplicity. Consistency. Honesty. Resiliency. Humility. I have worked my ass off trying to adhere to these traits. My shaving mirror reality check: "Have I done the right things today?"

Simplicity is genius, someone wrote. I harp on the subject with the athletes I deal with, with my wife, with whoever will listen. (Which is sort of the case with everything I say, I guess.) Humanity has shot itself in its own foot (to say nothing about what it has done to the feet of others) throughout its history. I have not made any real attempt to disarm it. For the most part, I have followed Voltaire's advice and simply cultivated my own garden.

I have supported activist causes but never led any. I do not trust the judgments of mass man, as I said in a recent chapter. Someone once told me after a speech I delivered to a bunch of corporate suits, "You could be a dangerous man." I have not had any inclination toward danger, my own or others. I was chided by good old dad, "Your nose is not small kid, so you're going to have to work at keeping it clean." (*That* has not been a simple task.)

Consistency. Aside from the description NHL coach Pat Quinn gave when he introduced me to an intimidated acquaintance as "just a street bum with an education," the most flattering remark about me was made by a former major league player and hitting coach, Merv Rettenmund. My publisher put his testimonial on the front cover of one of my books. "In my 36 years in professional baseball (he's added a few since then), Harvey Dorfman is the most consistent person I have met." Well, he did not say consistently good or bad. Still, it helps to have others reinforce your attempt to 'get it right' in this life.

Honesty. My father's words to me were pragmatic rather than moralistic: "If you tell the truth, kid, you'll never have to try to remember what you said." I will take it a long step further. The ability to be honest is the ability to be fearless. A great restraint for people telling the truth, aside from their being liars who have very specific, self-serving agendas, is the fear that the remark is confrontational, insulting, provocative (it may be all of these) and will result in a negative—even hostile—response. But there is such a thing as diplomatic language. In my experience, *how* I said what I believed to be the truth has most often had more to do with the other person's response than *what* I said. So the truth can often hurt less than the style of presentation: language, timing, and tonality. However I have approached others, I have worked hard at being honest to my own self, first and foremost.

Resiliency. Bend but do not break is the sports metaphor. A dictionary would say that being resilient is having the ability to recover (snap back) from illness, misfortune or change. Interesting how, in this context, 'change' is a borderline pejorative. And that is significant. Many people do not handle change well. At this stage of my life, I must confess to hovering around that crowd. But when I was young, I courted change. Perhaps because my childhood was so predictably the same—day after day—in that sickbed. Whatever the impetus had been for my affinity for change, it allowed me to learn how to do something that defined me to a significant degree. To develop appropriate responses to whatever unanticipated events I met in my life.

The word 'response' is one I speak of with *all* my athletes. I say to them, "If you want to know who a person is, watch how he responds to adversity." Yes, to 'illness, misfortune and change.' Dealing effectively with the curve balls life throws at us (or we throw at ourselves) requires responses that are rational, rather than emotional. Responses that treat the issue in front of us, rather than what we wish the issue were. Or what a heightened state of agitation leads us to believe it is.

"It's not how many times you're knocked down," a famous football coach told his charges. "It's how many times you get up." Whether or not we respond well by snapping back. By being resilient.

Humility. My father again: "He who has a love affair with himself will have no competition." I cannot remember the first day he said that to me, but I can recall exactly where and when my sister, Dolly, first started her campaign to keep me humble. Of course, whatever braggadocio she saw in me was just an act. Compensation for a deflated ego that I inflated with the luxurious gas coming from the bullshit I spewed out as a kid. Dolly sang her song of sarcasm to me for the first time in the living room of our Reservoir Place apartment in the Bronx.

"You're just too marvelous, too marvelous for words. . ." (a Johnny Mercer song). She provoked dual responses. First, it irritated the shit out of me. Then the opposite, sort of. All she had to do was begin to hum, and I held whatever self-aggrandized b.s. was spewing forth from my inferior self.

A person who needs convincing that it behooves him to have humility might consider words of fourth century *Palestinian Talmud*: "Man was created on the sixth day so he could not be boastful, since he came after the flea in order of creation." Absent that warning, many of us boast because we are blinded and deafened by what I call our screaming needs.

I never really had grandiose longings. My ego focused more on preservation than greatness. I knew my limits. In college, I read and put into a notebook these words: "Every stink that fights the ventilator thinks it's Don Quixote." Clever. I have no idea who said that. (Sancho Panza?) But we all need to be proud of ourselves, in some way. We might try being proud in humility; proud in that we are not proud.

Reason has been more than just 'important' to me. It was all-too-easy for me to be emotional when I was a sick kid. But I was fortunate to have a restraint: my asthma. The more emotionally worked up I became, the more physically debilitated I became. My breathing was adversely affected by this state. If necessity can teach the bear to dance, it sure as hell taught me to back off feelings and expressions emanating from my emotional system. So reason acted as a harness on my irrational, emotional impulses. "Reason saved me from myself," as George Santayana has written.

Balance. "Nothing in excess," said the Greeks. I teach that the word 'too' is an enemy of balance. Too hot, too cold; too big, too small. Too much of a good thing becomes a bad thing, as homespun wisdom tells us. Our current society does not seem to adhere to that point of view. Wretched excess prevails. It is encouraged by those who benefit from adherence to the view. "The Golden Mean" of ancient times seems to be just that in today's word of instant gratification and extreme self-indulgence: ancient.

A few words about 'the inner self.' I do not imagine too many people walking by me on the street think about their personal reality. Thinking that the sole source of their reality is within them, rather than without. But I tell athletes to live that way—from the inside out, instead of from the outside in. A half hour (at least) is required to explain that thought.

Yet, plenty of bad stuff happens within. So we fight the battle on two fronts (at least). A character in *Man's Fate* (Malraux) hopes "to be stronger than what happens inside (him) at a particular moment." How does one fight that fight? The forces of good inside vs. the forces of bad inside. It is called conflicting impulses. I have them every day. Every hour? Not anymore. But I remember being a young man reading with great empathy the words of St. Augustine: "Lord, make me pure, but not yet." Speaking for myself, my needs have been satisfied, but I have not been made pure.

I have few regrets, but those I have are real and deep. I know the good I have done—and the bad. I am not a perfectionist but detest my imperfections. Am I happy? When asked that by a couple of students more than thirty years ago, I said, "Happiness isn't the point. Understanding is." Luckily, they didn't know what I was talking about, so that conversation ended there. And will here. The abstraction called 'happiness' has never been clear to be—or important. There have been many moments of extreme joy, and those I have felt clearly—and 'happily.'

Here I will attempt (for the sake of those beloved grandsons) to identify what I have written about before—and identified as 'common enemies.' Enemies of the person I have sought to be. Some of the battles have been won. Some lost. A few are still in progress.

The view that money is the compelling and controlling influence on a person's life. Never a real problem for me. When Anita, the kids and I moved to Vermont from Long Island, my teaching salary decreased dramatically. We made it work. Many Long Island faculty members said they wanted to do what I was doing. Right. They blamed their wives, not the value they put on money.

An inability to deal rationally with opposing ideas or dilemmas. Too much agonizing never brought a right decision, I learned. I trusted my instincts and intuition as well as my brain. Sometimes I was right.

A psychological yielding to physical infirmity or injury as self-identity. Welcome to my early world. In beating the instinct, I swung like a pendulum (as Anita reminds me quite often) to the other extreme, identifying myself exclusively by, as my doctor says ironically, a warrior "at war with (my) pathology." Tough-guy stupid, sometimes.

The delusion or rationalization that your circumstance is beyond your control and therefore unchangeable. Courage is required! (That's the title of a book I started to write and will never complete.) "Fight, fight against the burning of the light." Giving in—quitting—is unacceptable. The insistent will must prevail.

An excessive desire for comfort or ease. I behave ridiculously at times, so I have been told, to establish (to myself) that I will not value or yield to comfort. Too many years in the comfort and security of a sick bed. An exaggerated response. I'm still working on balance with this one.

The conflict of philosophies based on different values held within a group or corporation or family. As a subordinate, I have very often made my superiors uncomfortable, because I do not suffer fools easily. Or their arbitrary mandates. When I have had positions of authority, I have tried to be fair-minded. But I sure as hell was emphatic about how I wanted things done. Yes, I listened. But to thinking people, not griping people.

The habitual use of judgmental language. After I had been schooled in semantics, my learning precluded the baser instinct of labeling people. It is now an *absolute* no-no for me.

The conflict created by the need for instant gratification and the need for approval. Natural but naughty, in my book. The fates know I did all-too-much of this as a child trying to get his feet off the bed and onto the firm footing. I embarrassed myself (with my father's and sister's help) enough to have the tendency squelched. Smothered. Killed dead. I have an awful time responding well to praise, as a result. (I occasionally brag to Anita; who understands and forgives.)

A focus on uncontrollable results or consequences. That song lyric, "If they asked me, I could write a book"—I could on this subject. Much (I was tempted to say 'most') of my work with clients and family members has to do with this enemy. I have conquered it completely. *That's* bragging! Sorry.

An inability to trust yourself. I've lived long enough to win by default, if not by my own merit. But I really have come to the winning side of the ledger on this one. The trick is to work on developing a self to begin with. That has been a life's work for me. I have erred on the side of arrogance, but learned a valuable, if painful lesson as a result: There is a big difference between being G-O-O-D and being G-O-D. My mortal limitations were made abundantly clear to me. (In a particular circumstance, very painfully clear.)

The lack of zeal and vitality caused by loss of hope and motivation. To lose hope is to lose motivation. To have no motivation leads to having no energy or enthusiasm for life. Vitality: *vita* means life. I'll be a long time dead, I was told by guess-who. Breathing became a luxury. As long as I have had breath—and I only speak of what has happened to this point—I have valued life. 'Zeal' may seem to be a term too energetic to describe my inner self. But I am glad to wake up every day. (I'm glad to go to sleep also.)

The tendency to take personally all mistakes, criticism and failure at a task. That is the enemy professional athletes are confronting daily. Public failure can be a bear that wrestles the psyche to the ground. I intervene regularly in such fights. Criticism comes from coaches and managers, as well as from fans. Sometimes from spouses or other family members. To teach is to learn. The more I hear myself talk to these guys, the less likely I am to be victimized by the tendency. A good thing about old age: thicker skin.

Enough of that.

Though I have spoken so much about my father, lots about my sisters, less about my mother, little about Anita, Melissa and Dan, *all* are my life. I determined to avoid the personal aspects of lives that go on still. So I have spoken about influences of the past—anecdotes mostly, without getting sappy (I hope) about those who are so important in my life—most notably

Anita, Melissa, Dan and their families. Their limited appearance is based on privacy and contemporaneity, not lack of love and appreciation. While writing this memoir, I heeded the words of Creon to Antigone: "Go to the dead and love them."

Anita's dear cousin Dorothy (more like a sister to her) is now gone. As are Karl Kuehl, a good pal and the major catalyst for my career in baseball, and that wonderful man, Whitey Lockman. And speaking of wonderful, Coach Parker. They joined other family members and people who populated my inner world (Rosemary Clooney, Jo Stafford, John Fowles, John Updike, *et. al.*) in the passing parade. It is a procession of sadness.

But my re-discovered high school buddies, those from *earliest* times— Warren, Joel, Al, Ed and Kenny—are still around and alert. And surely, a good many others I cannot possibly list, all members of the variegated tribe of people who are very important to me. And Brockport's Vinnie Lista. Still here, and that's good.

John Fowles said that writing about one's past is impossible, but necessary. That being the case, what needed to be done has been done. The stories have been told. And that's that.

www.ingramcontent.com/pod-product-compliance
Lightning Source LLC
Chambersburg PA
CBHW030651110726
47901CB00002B/669